An Elephant's Swimming Pool

MALCOLM COX

DPI
DISCIPLESHIP
PUBLICATIONS
INTERNATIONAL

www.dpibooks.org

An Elephant's Swimming Pool
© 2007 by Discipleship Publications International
300 Fifth Avenue
Fifth Floor
Waltham, Massachusetts 02451

Printed in the United States of America.

ISBN-10: 1-57782-206-4
ISBN-13: 978-157782-206-6

Cover Design: Jennifer Maugel
Interior Design: Thais Gloor

To my wife, Penny.

John is known as "The Apostle of Love," but you are Dr. Love!

Twenty-two years together and counting.
I'm so glad I sold that French horn.

Contents

Preface 9

Introduction 11
An Elephant's Swimming Pool

Chapter 1...19
Can You Tell What It Is Yet?

Chapter 2...27
Whips and Wine

Chapter 3...35
Transformers

Chapter 4...43
Open Eye Surgery

Chapter 5...49
R-E-S-P-E-C-T

Chapter 6...59
Super-Sandwich

Chapter 7...69
Confusion and Refreshment

Chapter 8...75
Questions, Questions, Questions

Chapter 9...83
An Ophthalmologic Opportunity

Chapter 10...89
A Nation of Sheep-Keepers

Chapter 11...97
Die to Live Another Day

Chapter 12...105
Scent of Glory

Chapter 13 113
   Don't Forget Your Towel

Chapter 14 121
   Honeymoons and Cement Mixers

Chapter 15 129
   God the Gardener

Chapter 16 137
   Noddy and the Seal

Chapter 17 143
   The 1-2-3 of Prayer

Chapter 18 151
   The Trials of God and Men

Chapter 19 157
   The Book of the Film

Chapter 20 163
   Resurrection Restoration

Chapter 21 171
   Memorable Meals

Epilogue..181
   Sink or Swim?

Preface

I read somewhere that no one should write a book until they are over forty. How can anyone know anything worth passing on until they've lived a while? I don't know if that is a fair observation, but I crossed that barrier a few years ago and so have no more excuses.

So here is my first book. I hope you like it. Some of it was fun to write and some was jolly hard work. I am hopeful this book will inspire, challenge and encourage you, and I know that I am the richer for reading, thinking and writing about the Gospel of John.

A few words on getting the most out of this book...

My advice is to follow a four-step program:

1. Pray for insight before reading.

2. Read the relevant chapter of John's Gospel.

3. Think about it, asking yourself questions such as

   • What does this chapter teach me about God, Jesus, the Holy Spirit?
   • What might be the reason God wanted John to record this?
   • What did these events and/or words mean to the people in the passage?
   • What might be the message for me and those I love today?

4. Then and only then read the relevant chapter of my book.

Can I make a plea? As one who has done the very opposite, please can I, in all confessional humility, dissuade you from simply reading my book and not the Gospel? I am hoping you find my book interesting and helpful, but the power is in the Scriptures. John's writing has survived two millennia. I doubt mine will last quite that long!

The basic idea of this book is to help daily devotions, although it could be used in a number of other contexts for teaching or group study. I envision people reading John chapter 1, reading chapter 1 of my book, making some notes in a journal, and using the prayer at the end of each chapter as a starting point for their own prayers. However, I am very happy for this book to be used in any way that benefits the reader. So if you want to read one chapter a day or one a week—that is fine by me.

And finally…if anything I have written helps you or anyone you know, please drop me a line through my publisher.[1] You never know, if I get enough positive responses, I might write another book.

Happy reading,

Malcolm

---

1. Send emails to info@dpibooks.org

Introduction

An Elephant's Swimming Pool

In the midst of frantic, screaming, over-the-top fans at sports events or rock concerts, we have all seen a person in the middle of all the din of excitement, calmly holding a sign to catch the attention of the roving TV cameras—neatly or not-so-neatly lettered with the following message: "John 3:16."

Perhaps you think you know what John 3:16 says.

I was once severely embarrassed when Doug, a good friend of mine, asked me to quote it. I had a thorough church upbringing (choir, youth group, confirmation classes...the lot) and thought this would be a walk in the park. I failed miserably ("For God so loves...no...loved us...no...the world that he gave...no...sent his only...no...one and only Son that...no...so...Oh, I give up!). I cut Doug from my Christmas card list after that.

Can you quote it word for word right now? Go on. Try writing it down:

_____

_____

_____

_____

_____

_____

Check below to see if you got it right (the NIV or King James version, anyway).[1]

So how did you do? Want some good news? Your salvation does not depend on an exact quote! But this is a well-known verse for a good reason. It summarizes the gospel, the "good news," in just a few words.

John's Gospel is probably read more than Mark's, Matthew's or Luke's. *(Sorry, guys. Not really fair is it, considering you three wrote yours earlier, and John came onto the scene as a Johnny-come-lately! But as you each pointed out, Jesus said that the first would be last and the last first, right?)* (See Matthew 19:30, Mark 10:31, Luke 13:30.)

Why is John's account so popular? I do not know all the reasons, but there has been recognition of its universal appeal from early times. Augustine (354–430 AD) is reported as saying:

> John's gospel is deep enough for an elephant to swim, and
> shallow enough for a child not to drown.

Now I've never seen an elephant's swimming pool (can you imagine the synchronized diving event from the high board at the elephant Olympics?!), but what I think he was trying to say is there is something for everyone in John's writings. I believe you will agree if you come with me for a swimming lesson in the Gospel of John.

Let's have two understandings as we progress through the book:

(1) You will read the corresponding chapter in John before reading my chapter. Any swimmer is wise to do some stretches and preparation before going after his or her strokes. I will not be quoting the verses, so you need to already be familiar with what John has said before you read what I say.

(2) This book is not a commentary, so I will not be looking at the chapters verse by verse. I will simply be giving a response that some part of the chapter evoked in me. You can ponder

---

1. "For God so loved the world that he gave his one and only Son, that whoever believes in him shall not perish but have eternal life." (NIV) "For God so loved the world, that he gave his only begotten Son, that whosoever believeth in him should not perish, but have everlasting life." (KJV)

some of the other parts of John's chapters yourself. Hopefully my comments will just be a "springboard" for your own thoughts.

Before diving in, let's take a look around this pool. Here is some background you might find interesting.

Whose Pool Is It?

John is not named as the author anywhere in the book, but there is specific evidence from outside the Bible that points to John—the son of Zebedee and brother to James. We know that Polycarp and Clement of Alexandria thought that it was written by John. These men were Christians writing in the second century AD. Polycarp said, "John the disciple of the Lord, who leaned back on his breast, published the Gospel while he was resident at Ephesus in Asia."[2] Clement of Alexandria said, "John, last of all…composed a spiritual Gospel."[3]

Within the book, there are intriguing clues to the author's identity.

- He saw the events firsthand (1:14, 2:11, 21:20–25) and was the "disciple whom Jesus loved" (21:20). He was there at the crucifixion (19:26, 35) and tomb (20:2, 8).

- This disciple was one of the Twelve (13:23), but not Peter, Philip, Thomas, Judas Iscariot or Judas son of James—since these are all named in chapters 13 to 16.

- John was one of the "inner circle" of three (Peter, James and John) that often accompanied Jesus (Matthew 17:1; Mark 5:37, 13:3, 14:33; Luke 5:8–10).

- And lastly, how about a bit of educated speculation? He may well have been the other disciple of John the Baptist who was with Andrew in John 1:35–42. As Andrew went to find his brother, Peter, perhaps John went to tell his brother, James, about this amazing teacher.

2. Polycarp lived 69–156 AD and had been a disciple of John. He is quoted by Irenaeus in his *Adversus Haereses* 3.1.2, writing in about 180 AD.

3. Clement of Alexandria lived about 150–215 AD. He is quoted by Eusebius in his *Historia Ecclesiastica* 6.14.7. Eusebius lived from about 270 to 340 AD.

There seems little doubt this elephant's swimming pool has "Made by John" stamped on the bottom.

Where Was the Pool Built?

We know John lived in Ephesus for some time. Irenaeus says, "The church in Ephesus was founded by Paul, and John remained among them permanently until the time of Trajan."[4] Polycarp (an elder who knew John) said, as quoted earlier, "John the disciple of the Lord, who leaned back on his breast, published the Gospel while he was resident at Ephesus in Asia."[5] Look on the bottom of the pool again and you'll see "Made in Ephesus" clearly written next to "Made by John."

Who Was the Pool Built For?

Being written in Ephesus might mean the book was intended for the church there, but more likely John had a wider audience in mind since there are no specific references to Ephesus in the Gospel. It seems he was writing mostly to Jews and God-fearers (Gentiles who were attracted to Judaism) scattered after the destruction of the Temple in 70 AD (see more below). This presented John with an ideal evangelistic opportunity. He filled the void left for the Jews by the destruction of their entire religious system. They were asking themselves, now that the Temple has gone, how and where do we worship and sacrifice? Where are our priests? Where is our God?!

The Gospel answers these questions by relocating the focus onto Jesus. He is worthy of worship, he is our great High Priest, he is the sacrifice we need (the Lamb of God), he is God in the flesh.

When Was It Built?

The Gospel of John was probably written after Peter's death, which was around 65 AD (this makes sense of John 21:19). It was possibly also written after the destruction of the temple in 70 AD. This seems likely because John emphasizes the way Jesus replaces the Temple and Jewish feasts (as we'll see in the chapters to follow).

---

4. Irenaeus in his *Adversus Haereses* book 3, writing in about 180 AD.
5. *Adversus Haereses* 3.1.2.

There are reasons to believe the Gospel was written in the reign of the Roman Emperor Domitian. He minted coins on which he was identified as *Dominus et Deus* (Latin for "Lord and God"). This is the very same phrase used by Thomas to describe Jesus in John 20:28. In choosing to quote Thomas, John might be offering a not-too-subtle "dig" at Domitian and reminding the Christians who is the true Lord! If this pool had a "DOB" stamped on it, it would probably say "Born in the 80s."

Why Was the Pool Built?

As mentioned earlier, John saw a window of opportunity for the evangelization of Jews and God-fearers who were questioning their faith after the destruction of the Temple. He clearly states his reasons in John 20:30–31:

> Now Jesus did many other signs in the presence of his disciples, which are not written in this book. But these are written so that you may come to believe that Jesus is the Messiah, the Son of God, and that through believing you may have life in his name. (NRSV)

The Greek translation of the phrase "so that you may come to believe" is subtle and can also be translated "so that you may continue to believe." Was the Gospel written to convert nonbelievers or to inspire perseverance in believers? My guess is yes...to both! As Augustine indicated, this pool is shallow enough for spiritual searchers and young Christians, but deep enough for seasoned saints who swim in it over and over again, always learning more.

In Conclusion

I do not know if you like swimming (not my favorite pastime), but there is no doubting it can improve your health. In this Gospel-Pool there are spiritual health benefits as well.

1. You can learn to swim. I didn't enjoy learning to swim (the lungs full of chlorinated water and the sadistic swimming instructor who threw us into the deep end probably didn't help), but at least I am safe if I fall off a boat. You may not be sure what you believe in, but if you want to know what Jesus is all about you cannot do better than listen to his friend John—someone who knew him personally. I encourage you to sign up for swimming lessons. What you learn could save your life.

2. You can learn to swim better. My friend Cam (disgustingly good swimmer and surfer) took me to a local pool and showed me how to rotate my shoulders properly, push the water down the length of my body, and kick my legs efficiently to go faster. I'm still not very good, but at least I can go faster than I used to. Your faith may be alive, but is it growing? Why not see what John can teach you about Jesus, the Father and the Holy Spirit? Maybe it is time to be trained and taught by a disciple who actually walked with Jesus. Maybe it is time for a growth spurt.

3. You can learn to swim long-distance. What is the farthest you've ever swum? I did fifty widths for charity once. It took half a day because I had to stop after every two widths to catch my breath. I don't remember what the charity was (it was a long time ago), but I do remember the feeling of achievement at the end. Have you been flagging? Does the Christian life seem more of a drain than a joy? Why not see what John's Gospel can do for your spirit? Come and learn from one who went the distance. From what we know about John, he was the last apostle to die. He may well have been eighty or ninety years old when he left this earth. He was swimming till the end—and that is how I want to be.

Come on. Let's go for a swim together. I promise you will not drown. Jesus is an expert lifesaver!

Questions for Reflection
1. What do you want to learn from this Gospel about Jesus, the Father and the Holy Spirit?
2. What do you want to learn about yourself?

3. What are you most afraid of discovering?
4. What could be the best thing that might happen as a result of reading this book?

Prayer

Father, thanks for giving John the energy and inspiration to write his Gospel. Help me today to take the plunge and enjoy the swim. Help me trust you to choose the depth you know I can handle. I know you'll never let me drown. I want to swim and I want to make it to the other side. In Jesus' name, Amen.

1

Can You Tell What It Is Yet?

John Chapter 1

I have put off writing this opening chapter for as long as I can. Almost all the other chapters are written, but now it is time to grasp the nettle. I wonder if John had the same problem. Perhaps he received the same advice I did about writing essays at school. I was always told to write the introduction after completing the main body and conclusion of the essay. I can imagine John thinking, "I know how to end the book. I know what happens during the story. I know the signs I want to highlight and the teachings I want to record. But how on earth do I start this thing?"

Perhaps then he asked himself, "How did God start his record of his dealings with his creation?" John's mind casts back to Genesis; he contemplates the beginning of all things temporal and then has a flash of insight. "I know," he thinks, "I'll make the link between Jesus and creation." Then he sits down to write the parallel to Genesis 1:1 with the words, "In the beginning…" (John 1:1).

The goal of what I think John is doing with his Gospel is to present a stunning portrait of Jesus. He is an artist painting on a huge canvas with eye-catching broad strokes and yet with incredible subtlety. In this sense he is somewhat like Rolf Harris.[1] For those of you blissfully ignorant of Rolf, he is an Australian entertainer (recently awarded a CBE by the Queen[2]). One of his skills is painting on a large scale. When I was a kid he came to the town where I lived. He stood on the back of a flatbed lorry on which had been erected an

---

1. Rolf Harris has rarely been accused of subtlety!
2. Companion of the British Empire

enormous canvas. Dipping a twelve-inch brush into industrial-size tins of paint, he splashed paint onto the canvas.

Now and again he paused, stepped back from the developing picture and shouted his catchphrase, "Can you tell what it is yet?" All the other children and I yelled back our suggestions, which were invariably wrong. Finally—splish, splash, splosh—with three quick stokes of the brush the whole picture took shape. We all gasped in amazement (well, we were very young!) to see how virtually complete the picture had been and yet how impossible it had been for us to tell what it was before the final strokes had been applied.

Look at That!

Now I may be stretching the analogy a little thin between the apostle John and Rolf Harris CBE, but I reckon John is building a picture with chapter one that makes sense of the rest of the Gospel. His descriptions of Jesus as existing before time began (1:1–2), being God (1:1, 14, 18), and being the author of creation (1:3, 10—see also Acts 3:15, Hebrews 1:1–3) are a stunning introduction to the identity of Jesus. Not content with that, John goes on to tell us that in Jesus we have seen God (v18)—something that had never before occurred. His readership was aware Jesus had not been universally accepted (understatement!), and John gives the context for this by emphasizing that he was the light shining in an unwelcoming darkness (1:5, 8:12, 9:5—see also Matthew 5:14–16).

Jesus is also presented as the one to give us the true light (1:9) as opposed, presumably, to the fake light of false religion peddled by many. Not only that, but he is here to provide the way to become children of God (1:12–13) as well as to provide multiple blessings (1:16), grace and truth (1:17) and the way to know God (1:18). That's a pretty impressive CV! John is saying, "Look at that! I have never seen anything like that. You've never seen anything like that. *No one in the history of history has seen anything like that!*"

The question worth asking ourselves is whether we have become so accustomed to reading, thinking, hearing and singing about Jesus that the "Wow!" factor has worn away. In reading John 1 we are hearing from someone who had lived as a disciple for decades, yet had lost none of his fervor. I want to be like that. Rereading and praying through this passage and meditating on its content will surely help.

Don't Look at Me

Both Jesus and John the Baptist were executed. It seems that within first-century Judaism John the Baptist was a more famous "martyr" than Jesus. John didn't let anyone down, but Jesus did. John appeared radical yet orthodox. Jesus appeared radical and blasphemous! Imagine travelling back in time to Palestine in the first century. You find an average Israelite and ask him or her about Jesus. You might get a puzzled look. But ask about John the Baptizer and you would most likely get instant connection. His "brand recognition" worked really well. John was the one baptizing hordes of people in the Jordan and then had his head chopped off by the corrupt King Herod. It is because of his teaching and ministry that we find people still holding to his view of baptism in Acts 19. They are following the teachings of a national hero.

The apostle John was aware that the evangelistic thrust of his Gospel would be compromised if people didn't understand the Baptist's true role as a herald to Jesus. Hence, we find John the Baptist emphasizing again and again that he was *not* the Messiah (1:20–21). In addition, he goes out of his way to make it clear that the purpose of his own mission (1:31) was to point out Jesus as the true Messiah (1:26–27, 29, 34, 36).

John the Baptist was quick to say to people, "Don't look at me; look at him." There is a lesson in this for us. John combined great boldness with great humility. A tough combination. Not many handle this balance very well. I am more inclined to equate quietness with humility. How often have you heard it said, "She's so humble; she never draws attention to herself"? Normally this means something like, "She's so quiet. It must be because she is really humble." But is this always the case? It is true that humility can be demonstrated by holding one's tongue, but it is also true that someone speaking up for truth when it is difficult can show genuine humility.

Jesus himself, of course, is a great example of boldness and humility combined. He knew when to speak and when to be silent, yet he was always humble in either situation. Perhaps the point for us is to not make assumptions about loud-mouthed people and quiet-as-a-mouse people. The question is not one of volume, but of how successfully one points to Jesus. This is true of words *and* deeds. The poem "I'd Rather See a Sermon" stings in just the right way:

I'd rather see a sermon than hear one any day;
I'd rather one should walk with me than merely tell the way.
The eye's a better pupil and more willing than the ear,
Fine counsel is confusing, but example's always clear;
And the best of all the preachers are the men who live their
    creeds,
For to see good put in action is what everybody needs.
I soon can learn to do it if you'll let me see it done;
I can watch your hands in action, but your tongue too fast
    may run.
And the lecture you deliver may be very wise and true,
But I'd rather get my lessons by observing what you do;
For I might misunderstand you and the high advice you give,
But there's no misunderstanding how you act and how you
    live.[3]

Preachers like myself need to read that poem regularly, but then so do all who profess the Christian faith. We are all walking, talking representatives of Jesus Christ. "D. L. Moody claimed that in any group of 100 people, only one will be reading the Bible, while 99 read the Christians."[4] John the Baptist successfully pointed to Jesus and fulfilled his calling from God because he spoke boldly and lived humbly.

Look at the Results

The upshot of all this is that people followed Jesus. I think that is one of the things John wants us to see from this chapter. After all,

---

3. *Collected Verse of Edgar Guest* (New York: Buccaneer Books, 1976), 599.
4. Sarah Tillet, "Community and Our Inheritance," *Caring for Creation* (Oxford: The Bible Reading Fellowship, 2005), 111–112.

those of us who sing "I Have Decided to Follow Jesus" ask ourselves from time to time whether we can persevere in "no turning back." And people who are contemplating following Jesus ask the question, "What does it mean to follow him?" Apostle John says, "Follow the eternal one made flesh." Baptist John says, "Follow the one here to take away your sin." Both say, "Follow and be amazed." What is it that we see in the lives of those who follow and humbly point to Jesus? We see that others join in following him.

Leading others to follow Jesus as they themselves follow him is something that links humble leaders and humble followers. Both are good at inspiring people to follow the right people. After John the Baptist points to Jesus, two disciples (Andrew and, many think, the author of the Gospel, John himself) follow him (1:35–39). Andrew is sufficiently impressed with Jesus after a day's acquaintance to recommend him to his brother Simon (1:40–42). "Pointer" John the Baptist has been imitated by "pointer" Andrew. The newest follower becomes the next "pointer." In the next scene we see Philip signed up by Jesus. What happens next? Philip himself trots off to tell Nathanael about Jesus and he too signs up for the swim.

Being a follower of Christ is not about being passive. We are in his discipleship school being trained and transformed. The joy of finding the light, knowing the living God, and having our sins taken away is too wonderful not to be shared. Someone once said that the test of being a leader isn't whether you have certificates, positional authority or a title, but simply to look behind and see if anyone is following. The test of a follower who has been given "the right to become [a child] of God" (1:12) must include passing on the good news and becoming a "pointer." This is a humble job. You don't get the glory. But you do share the joy.

So who can you point to Jesus today? Is there a friend who could profit from a little prod into Jesus' path? If you are a follower, that is part of your job. If you are a leader, ditto. Not as a duty or a chore, but rather as a joy. I imagine John the Baptist couldn't keep his hand by his side once he saw Jesus and realized who he was. His arm shot out and his fingers pointed directly and excitedly at Jesus as the words flew out of his mouth, "Look, the Lamb of God!" (1:36).

I hope reading through and thinking about this amazing chapter of John's Gospel has helped awaken or reawaken your astonishment about Jesus. Perhaps the picture is clearer, bigger, more colorful. I'm sure if you persevere with this book and continue deeper into the waters of John's Gospel you will find some aspects of the Christ that astonishes you all the more.

I leave you with the lyrics of one of my favorite hymns, "You're the Word of God the Father":

You're the word of God the Father,
From before the world began;
Every star and every planet,
Has been fashioned by your hand.
All creation holds together,
By the power of your voice;
Let the skies declare your glory,
Let the land and sea rejoice!

Chorus
You're the author of creation, You're the Lord of every man;
And your cry of love rings out across the lands.

Yet you left the gaze of angels,
Came to seek and save the lost;
And exchanged the joy of heaven,
For the anguish of a cross.
With a prayer you fed the hungry,
With a word you stilled the sea.
Yet how silently you suffered,
That the guilty may go free.

Chorus
You're the author of creation, You're the Lord of every man;
And your cry of love rings out across the lands.

With a shout you rose victorious,
Wresting victory from the grave,
And ascended into heaven,
Leading captives in your wake.
Now you stand before the Father,
Interceding for your own.
From each tribe and tongue and nation,
You are leading sinners home.

Chorus
You're the author of creation, You're the Lord of every man;
And your cry of love rings out across the lands.[5]

Questions for Reflection

1. What part of John's description of Jesus do you connect with most? Why?
2. What can you do to recapture or deepen your "Wow!" factor when thinking about Jesus?
3. Would friends regard you as a humble follower-pointer or leader-pointer of people to Jesus? Why or why not?
4. Why not take some special time to sing the above song to God? If you don't know the tune, you could make up your own (or find it on the Internet).

Prayer

Father, when I forget why I have started swimming, take me back to the beginning. Never let go of me when I let go of my reasons for following. Give me strength to point to your Son despite my weakness and sin. Use me to bring others to know this wonderful Word. In Jesus' name, Amen.

5..Keith Getty and Stuart Townend, "Across the Lands You're the Word of God." © 2002 Thank You Music. All rights reserved. Reprinted by permission.

2

Whips and Wine

John Chapter 2

First times are significant, aren't they? I remember my first kiss, the first time I danced with my wife, the first time I saw my first child (Lydia) at her birth, the first steps taken by my son (Fred), the first person I baptized (my fiancée, now my wife) and finishing my first book (this one!).

Make your own list. I remember the first time I _____. Fill in the blanks for yourself. I am sure it will be a litany of some of the most memorable experiences of your life.

Being alone for those experiences is less powerful than if you shared them with someone. It is like the old story of the golf-mad preacher. He wakes up one Sunday morning to the sight of the most beautifully sunny golf-perfect day, rings his assistant to say (with a suitably croaky voice), "I've got laryngitis. Could you preach today?" then packs his clubs for the course.

Peter speaks to God in heaven and says, "We've got to punish him, Lord."

God says, "Just you watch!"

The preacher tees off at the first hole and gets a hole-in-one—something he's never done before. He whoops with glee.

As Peter looks on, he says to God, "That's not much of a punishment."

God says with a twinkle in his eye, "But who can he tell?"

What's the Point?

Jesus performs his first miracle in a public place for the benefit of others. Those who benefited were the wedding guests (more and better wine leading to great celebration) and his own disciples (more and deeper faith leading to great trust).

Jesus must have known for a long time that he was destined to perform miracles, or more significantly perhaps for John, signs. I don't buy all those apocryphal stories of Jesus doing miracles as a kid. Turning clay into sparrows not only has no style; it has no point. No one needed to see such a thing. The real miracles were performed to help people either trust him and his message or to communicate something powerful about the heart, character and compassion of God (John 14:11, Acts 2:22). It's not that Jesus was an exhibitionist (cue a comparison with some famous illusionists who like to hang around in Perspex boxes and tanks of water), but he did miracles for a reason. They were designed to have an impact on someone. Sometimes it was a crowd, sometimes opponents, sometimes disciples, sometimes individuals—sometimes all of the above! The point is "impact." In fact, if Jesus had a name for his school of ministry it might have been "Impact School of Ministry."[1]

Why the Reluctance?

Perhaps the fact that his miracles were done for a specific purpose helps to explain his apparent reluctance to do what his mother asked (vv3–5). Of course, in the text his mother doesn't actually ask him to do anything, but since a mother knows her son better than anyone else, I think it is reasonable to suppose she knew he was able to do something about the situation and hoped he would. I wonder whether the translators' punctuation does this sentence justice. I'm not sure she said it like this with a full stop at the end: "They have no more wine." I reckon it was more like, "They have no more wine…" dot, dot, dot, with a knowing look in her eye! The time isn't right, the audience isn't ready, the sign isn't necessary, but then it appears Jesus recognizes that this is an opportunity not to be missed.

---

1. Incidentally I have also come across a London driving school called "The Impact School of Motoring"—I'm not so sure that's a great name for a firm claiming to teach you how to drive. Perhaps they specialize in teaching people how to crash successfully?

Perhaps he has a *carpe diem* epiphany, and the Spirit prompts him to see the significance of the moment. All of a sudden he realizes that his mother's question is opening up a God-given opportunity.

Could it be that things start to come together in his head? Sitting there at a wedding feast he remembers the promised Messianic wedding banquet long anticipated in Jewish tradition (applied to Jesus himself in Matthew 22:1–14 and Revelation 19:9).[2] The water prefigures for him the waters of new life and rebirth (John 3:16, 7:38, Titus 3:5, Revelation 21:6), and the wine foreshadows the new wine bringing in the new covenant (Matthew 26:29, Mark 2:22, 1 Corinthians 11:25). He looks around at the guests, his mother and then his disciples. He realizes—it is time. Time to let them see the first sign. So he summons the servants…and the rest is history.

It's All in the Timing

Maybe the first miracle happened as I described and maybe not. But the point is that Jesus seized the opportunity in an unlikely situation to reveal his glory to his disciples, and they put their faith in him (v11). The question that comes to my mind is this: Do I recognize God's timing? I love the fact that Jesus' first sign was done at a party. It wasn't done at the temple (more on that in a minute), or on a mountaintop in front of a huge crowd with Herod, the Pharisees, Sadducees, teachers of the Law, Nicodemus, Pilate and the high priest all in attendance. Also, it is not the sort of miracle I would expect from a Messiah. Jesus did a behind-the-scenes miracle in an obscure village to the benefit of others and blessed the bride and groom on their special day without stealing the limelight.

I wonder whether I, and perhaps some of you reading this book, miss many of God's "opportunity-moments" because we have assumed how he works. We think he works at certain times in certain places in certain ways. How do we know how and when he works? He worked by impregnating a virgin (Luke 1:30–37). He worked through the execution of the only perfect man (2 Corinthians 5:21). He worked in a dead womb and with sperm from a man as good as dead (Romans 4:19). He worked through a rebellious

---

2. Others like John the Baptist (John 3:27–30) and Paul (Ephesians 5:25–33) also saw Jesus as a bridegroom.

prophet (Jonah 1:3, 10, 12). He worked through a Christian-killer (Acts 7:57–60, 8:3, 1 Timothy 1:13). He worked through a prostitute (Joshua 6:25). He worked through a fallen hero (Judges 16:23–31). He worked through leaders who felt they weren't ready for the job (Exodus 3:11, Joshua 1:6–9, Judges 6:15–16). He worked through people who were too young (1 Samuel 16:11–13, Daniel 1). He worked through people who were too old (Luke 1:18 –19).

What is the "too" thing for you? Do you think of yourself as too ill, old, young, undisciplined, emotional, boring, sinful, ungifted, fearful, uneducated or poor to be used by God? Or what about the people around you who you think are not possibly going to be open to the gospel? Do you think of them as too proud, steeped in sin, closed, irreligious, bitter, antagonistic, religious, foreign, wealthy, educated, uneducated, illiterate or busy? I have a verse for you to meditate on:

> "What is impossible with men is possible with God." (Luke 18:27)

Why not make a commitment to pray with faith for some of those "impossible" things and see what *God* can do that *we* cannot?

Magnet or Market?

Why do we have the wedding wonder-wine story followed by the temple table-turning story? In the former Jesus contributes to the celebrations of joyful people in an understated way. In the latter he is a confrontational troublemaker upsetting people in a very public way. Perhaps John is showing us two parts of the character of Jesus. The person who loved a party and the person who hated hypocrisy.

Why is Jesus so upset when he enters the temple? Why make a whip? Why throw his weight around? Answers vary. It appears that this trade of selling animals for sacrificing previously took place outside the temple and had only recently moved inside. The issue is not perhaps the trade, but where it took place. The place in question was the court of the Gentiles. This was an area set aside for Gentiles seeking God to "reach out for him and find him" (Acts 17:27) as Paul says to his very Gentile Athenian audience. Israel tended to forget the evangelistic mandate given them by God in general and located in the temple specifically. Consider the words of Solomon in dedicating the temple:

> "As for the foreigner who does not belong to your people Israel but has come from a distant land because of your name—for men will hear of your great name and your mighty hand and your outstretched arm—when he comes and prays toward this temple, then hear from heaven, your dwelling place, and do whatever the foreigner asks of you, *so that all the peoples of the earth may know your name and fear you,* as do your own people Israel, and may know that this house I have built bears your Name." (1 Kings 8:41–43, emphasis mine)

God has *al*ways had a heart for *all* peoples (Isaiah 49:6, 66:18–19), and the early Christians eventually grasped this (Acts 13:46–48) once Peter had wrapped his head around the happenings of Acts 10 and 11. Jesus was incensed by what was the effective exclusion of the Gentiles from their opportunity for access to God. He was the living, breathing, passionate lost-loving heart of God and could not stand to see barriers erected where bridges should have been built. The temple was designed to be a magnet, but instead became a market.

Walking and Talking

Now we come to John's commentary on this incident. He records that later, after the resurrection, the disciples remembered what Jesus had said. At that point, we presume, they got the point of what Jesus was doing here with his whip. At the time they were impressed with his zeal, but later they recognized that this sign was Jesus' way of indicating that he was going to not just temporarily clear the temple, but to *replace* it. Like many things to do with the new covenant, a spiritual reality replaces a physical reality that was only designed to point to that spiritual reality in the first place (Colossians 2:17). Christ came to invite all to experience the indwelling of God that begins in this life with the deposit of the Holy Spirit and is fully realized in the next life (Revelation 21:3). The "building" that matters in this life is not made of bricks and mortar, but of flesh and Spirit. We are individually (1 Corinthians 6:19, 2 Corinthians 6:16) and collectively the temple of God:

> In him the whole building is joined together and rises to become a holy temple in the Lord. And in him you too are being built together to become a dwelling in which God lives by his Spirit. (Ephesians 2:21–22)

The church (the body of Christ) and the fabric of the church (the individual Spirit-filled Christians) are the greatest possible witnesses to the world of God's magnificence. It is crucial to our witness and crucial to the witness of God that we take seriously our call to be the temple of God. Perfection is not demanded, but faithfulness is and ongoing repentance where it is needed. I don't believe the world is looking for a place that is problem-free (because they'll not fit in there), but a place of authenticity. In other words, a place where the talk and the walk match. The temple in Jerusalem claimed to be and was set up to be the location where the faithful could worship God and the seeking could find God. Its witness was compromised because pragmatism overtook spiritual priorities. Woe to us if we make the same mistake.

How can we tell if we are in danger of this? Consider these questions.

Questions for Reflection
1. Are cattle, sheep, coins and doves cluttering up your worship space? In other words, is there space in your life for God to move? Can you hear his voice? Are you making time to pray and read his word?

2. Can the "Gentiles" get a clear look at God when they observe the way you live? Are you living with the light at full power, or is the dimmer switch in operation? (See Matthew 5:14–16.)
3. Does Jesus need to get out his whip? If so, what would he want to sweep out of your life?
4. Is there something you consider "impossible" for God? Why not once again take up the challenge to pray for God to not just make wine, but the best wine that has ever been tasted?

Prayer

Father, thank you for the humility and servant heart of Jesus. I'm grateful to see that he wants people to be happy and enjoy life. Give me the faith to trust you for all the things outside my control and to grow to believe that you can do more than I can ask or imagine. I do not want anything in my life that stops people from seeing your glory. I want to be a worthy ambassador for you and a pure temple of the Holy Spirit. Give me strength to resist distraction and sin. If you need to make another whip, help me to welcome the discipline and not resent it. May my zeal remind others of the zeal of Christ. In his name I pray, Amen.

3

Transformers

John Chapter 3

When you were a kid did you have one of those transformer toys? You know the sort of thing—a car that became a robot if you twisted the chassis, folded the wheels and extended the exhaust. In my experience, transforming the one into the other takes twenty minutes for the average adult and twenty seconds for the average child. But have these toys *really* been transformed, or have they just achieved a different shape?

I see this as a parable of our times. Many want, seek, yearn for transformation but settle for reshaping. Plastic surgery changes the shape of the nose, but not the heart. Diet and exercise routines change the amount of fat you carry, but not the amount of sin, guilt or pain you carry. Many people want change, but do they want transformation? This is an urgent question both outside and inside the church.

Okay, let me be honest. I am asking these questions of myself as well as you, my dear reader. If you are a seeker after God's meaning and purpose for your life, are you prepared for radical transformation or are you just looking for "improvement"? What about if you are part of the church? Do you want Christ-like transformation or do you just want to be a "stronger Christian"? What about if you are part of church leadership? We can change the outward appearance of church (name, leadership structures, styles of worship, etc.), but do our congregations see these things as the *substance* of change, or are these things what they ought to be—symptoms of a deeper transformation?

I am making an assumption here and it may not be a fair one, but I think we'd better clear it up now or the rest of this book is not likely to have the impact either you or I hope it will. I want you to get value for your money and time! You see, I think John recorded this strange conversation between Jesus and Nicodemus right here near the start of his Gospel because, at least in part, he wanted the radical nature of encountering Jesus to be part of the fabric of his account of the life of Jesus. By the time John wrote this down the churches had been going for about fifty years. That's a long time. I reckon people then were a lot like people now. Once you get familiar with something, it starts losing its impact.

Christians then and Christians now struggle with the same things in understanding the impact Jesus Christ is supposed to have on their lives. We become Christians and experience a huge transformation in our thinking, our beliefs and our lifestyle (what the Bible calls repentance[1]). All good. But after a while there is a temptation (a strong one!) to get comfortable. This is death to a disciple. It is vital to our spiritual health to not lose sight of the fact that a relationship with God through Christ is one of ongoing transformation. By recording this Nico/Jesus interview, John is reminding the first-century Christians they mustn't lose sight of the fact that transformation is what it's about. And the Holy Spirit made sure this got into the canon so we wouldn't forget either.

So, back to my assumptions. I'm assuming you're up for some transformation. I'm assuming (hoping) that's why you bought this book. It's certainly why I've written it! Let's look at the time Nicodemus and Jesus had a chat and see what we can learn about true transformation.

In the Dark

I have to admit I feel sorry for Nicodemus—coming to Jesus for answers and only seeming to get questions. Jesus appears to be rather hard on poor old Nico. Perhaps this is to do with Nicodemus

---

1. See Ed Anton's excellent book for a more in-depth study of the subject: *Repentance: A Cosmic Shift of Mind and Heart* (Waltham, Mass: DPI, 2005).

himself, and perhaps it is partly to do with who or what Nicodemus represents. Why does he come to Jesus at night? The only other character in the Gospel to do that is Judas (18:1–3). Is John drawing a parallel? John makes a big deal of the theme of light and darkness in his Gospel (as we'll see), and I suspect this detail here is significant. It points to the ironic tragedy that both Nicodemus and Judas came to Jesus—the Light (1:4–10, 3:19–21, 8:12, 9:5)—in the dark. And in different ways, they *remained* in the dark. (It is encouraging to note that Nicodemus seems to have seen the light by John 19:38–42. Sometimes the light dawns later.)

In a culture where darkness was debilitating, John's readers would have caught the significance of this profound reality (those of us in the instant-flick-a-switch-for-light culture of the developed world cannot relate). Darkness is the place where confusion reigns (just remember the last time you got up in the middle of the night and trod on the cat). Let's see how this confusion plays out.

Man, Oh Man

As you probably know, the chapter divisions in our Bibles didn't exist in the original manuscripts. Most of the time this doesn't hinder the text, but here's one example where it obscures something interesting. Have a look at the end of chapter 2 and the start of chapter 3:

> But Jesus would not entrust himself to them, for he knew all men. He did not need man's testimony about man, for he knew what was in a man. Now there was a man of the Pharisees named Nicodemus.... (John 2:24–3:1)

What do you notice? Does anything stand out? I'll set it out again in a different way with my own emphasis,

> But Jesus would not entrust himself to them, for he knew all *men.*
> He did not need man's testimony about
> *man,*

for he knew what was in a
man.
Now there was a
man
of the Pharisees named Nicodemus...

In other words, Nicodemus is a man like any other. He is a person with no greater significance before God than you, me or any other man or woman on this planet—living or dead. What Jesus says to Nicodemus is what he says to everyone. This is significant because Nicodemus is "Israel's teacher" (3:10) and as such we might think Jesus' conversation with this theologian might not apply to us. Nothing could be further from the truth. As you read this chapter of John, it is worth stopping and asking yourself, "If I were having this conversation with Jesus, what would he say to me?" Just because you're not a Bible expert doesn't mean your understanding of salvation, rebirth and the Kingdom of God cannot be challenged, stretched, developed and matured.

Teachers Need Teaching

On the flip side of this, there does seem to be a specific challenge to Nicodemus in his role as a teacher. The sense of the original language seems to suggest not, "You are *one of* Israel's teachers," but more like, "You are *the* teacher of Israel" (my paraphrase of 3:10). This would make sense of the fact his name is mentioned again in John 7:50. If he were the pre-eminent teacher of Israel his position in our day would have been something like a melding together of a senior Bishop, a high court judge and a member of the cabinet. So be careful if you *do* know some Greek, have studied church history or hold a theology degree. To repeat the point of the previous paragraph in a different way: Just because you are a Bible expert doesn't mean your understanding of salvation, rebirth and the Kingdom of God cannot be challenged, stretched, developed and matured.

His confusion (emphasized by the repeated questions, "How can a man be born when he is old?" and "How can this be?") doesn't seem to get resolved. This is contrasted in the next chapter with the

Samaritan woman. She is racially ostracized (simply by being a Samaritan), should not even be allowed a conversation with a Rabbi (in that culture women did not talk to Rabbis), theologically confused (see the mountain argument—4:20), and morally suspect (five husbands down, another man in tow—4:18). Yet *she* is the one who finds resolution to all her questions. *Her* life is transformed, along with many other people, and the gospel spreads to a whole town (4:28–30, 39–42). Nicodemus doesn't get it; the Samaritan woman does.

Here is the point I think John wanted us to see: you may be a theological heavyweight or you may be a theological ignoramus, you may be morally and socially unimpeachable, or you may be morally and socially beyond the pale—but if you want to understand Jesus and if you want him to transform your life, you've got to do three things:

1. Keep listening to him even when the answers to your questions make no sense;
2. Keep the conversation going with him until you get the point;
3. Keep your heart open to him for change.

Or, put in a different way, humility wins over education.

Demolition Man

We don't just need fixing, mending or improving. The goal is not for us to live a good moral life. There *are* moral people outside the Kingdom of God. No, we need a complete rebuild, a total transformation. What does this take? First it takes demolishing the old life. That's why Jesus uses the image of rebirth. It's painful and messy.

Last year we planned to build a conservatory onto the back of our house. We had a cool vision of what it would look like. The building company drew up plans and we arranged the finances. One thing stood in the way—the old kitchen extension. I rented some sledgehammers I could hardly lift, bought a brazier, persuaded my friend Adrian to come over with his son, and we went to work.

Adrian and I with our teenage sons slaved for two whole days smashing, burning and making trips to the dump. It was exhausting, but it was also great fun (there's a strange delight in destroying something, isn't there?).

Once the rubble had been removed, the rubbish burned up and the ground levelled, the builders were able to come in and construct something that is so much better than what was there originally. The before-and-after pictures are astonishing. It hardly looks like the same house. Such is the impact of the gospel on our lives. This is the truth we must absorb—demolition comes before transformation. If we are willing, Jesus will take a sledgehammer to our lives...in a totally loving way, of course!

In the rest of John's Gospel we see Jesus taking sledgehammers to precious but badly constructed out-of-date ideas and teachings. Our old kitchen extension was dark and narrow, much like our pre-transformed way of thinking. Our conservatory is wide and light, much like our expanded and cleaned-out hearts. I know where I'd rather live—how about you?

Jesus gives Nicodemus a choice. "What's it to be, Nicodemus?" says Jesus. "The fulfilment of something you've dreamed of yet have never experienced—the reality of the prophecy in Ezekiel 36:25–27—or exclusion from the Kingdom of God? The reorientation of your assumptions by the one from heaven, or an existence in darkness?"

From the Pulpit

You may have noticed something. I've not mentioned the most famous part of this chapter, John 3:16. It is everywhere today—whitewashed onto motorway bridges, sprayed onto sheets and made into banners displayed at sports stadia. But do we have *any idea* of the radical nature of this statement? God is the sender, not the condemner. God is the giver, not the taker. God is the invader of darkness and evil in order to rescue us and bring us into light (1:4–9, 1 Peter 2:9–10). John 3:16 is *not* cute. It expresses a radical love that sent the Son to die for enemies. This was done not so we could have comfortable lives and a modicum of religiosity, but so we could be transformed into the likeness of Christ to God's glory, our joy and the world's astonishment.

Forgive my pulpiteering, but why can we not see this clearly? Why is it so many settle for passionless church-attending when a worshipful dynamic relationship with the Creator of *all that is seen and unseen* is available? Why fill up on junk food when "a feast is free"?[2] Mediocrity was never in the plan of God. Here is the joy of what I'm saying—it doesn't all depend on you. It's not that you must be transformed by your own power. Instead it's that we must allow God to do his work on us and in us, with our full and wholehearted cooperation. We are offered eternal life, we are offered new birth, we are offered transformation—settle for nothing less.

Questions for Reflection

1. What does transformation mean to you? How would you know you'd been transformed by God? What would it feel like? What would it look like?
2. Is there something Jesus needs to demolish in your life before something beautiful can be built in its place? What will it take for you to hand God the sledgehammer?
3. Will you commit yourself to transformation as we go through John's Gospel together?

Prayer

Father, I struggle with fear of change. Give me faith in place of fear. Help me trust your loving demolition and tender transformation. I want a heart that's always open to instruction. Reveal to me the assumptions I have about my faith that you need to challenge. Make me new and keep renewing me in the likeness of your Son. In Jesus' name, Amen.

2. From the old hymn "There Is Much to Do" by M. W. Spencer.

4

Open-Eye Surgery

John Chapter 4

I hate being stared at. An admiring gaze is fine. Envious glances are even okay. But suspicious, disapproving stares are a nightmare. I don't think Jesus had my problem, or if he did he coped with it well. He had to. Everywhere he went he did things and said things that made people stare at him. The Samaritan woman (we'll call her "Samantha" in this chapter, or "Sam" for short) was surprised that Jesus talked to her (v9), and the disciples were shocked to find him talking to a woman (v27). The local Samaritans were astonished to discover that this wandering Jewish Rabbi "really is the Savior of the world" (v42) and the royal official was amazed when he realized the timing of his son's healing (vv52–53).

Jesus did things deliberately to get attention. Not in the way children or insecure adults act up to make us pay them attention, but in such a way as to make a point. John emphasizes this point in the way he has told and arranged this story.

I am sure it is no coincidence that this "insignificant" Samaritan woman is sandwiched between the "important" religious leader (Nicodemus, 3:1) and the "important" political figure (the royal official, 4:46). Sam is the meat in the sandwich of the message. What is this message? Well it is multifaceted, but at least one part of it is that the life-changing, transformational message of the Messiah is available to all people. Some people get it and others don't. Indeed, it is often those we assume might be least open to the gospel that reveal themselves to be the most open. Have you noticed how Sam gets more airtime than Nicodemus? This is not what a first-century audience would have expected. Jesus breaks all the rules (and John highlights it) by talking to a woman…and a Samaritan one at that. During this time and culture men didn't talk to women in public and especially a man who was a Rabbi. The Samaritans were hated by the Jews (it was mutual) for various historical reasons. So what is going on?

Opening Eyes

Jesus loved opening things. He opened a tomb (John 11), a coffin (Luke 7:11–15), ears (Mark 7:33–35), heaven (Matthew 3:16), minds (Luke 24:45), mouths (Mark 7:35) and, of course, eyes (Mark 8:25, John 9:6–7). But most important of all, he opened hearts. Hearts need opening if they are going to be healed. Especially those that have been scarred by pain or blinded by prejudice—and Sam's heart suffered from both. We don't know all of what had happened in Sam's life, but it is fair to conclude that after five husbands and a lover, she must have had a good bit of pain in her heart. Turmoil might be a better word. The disciples noticed that she was the wrong race, the wrong gender, the wrong religion and had dodgy morals. They were prejudiced against talking to her. They saw her as avoidable. Jesus saw her as unmissable.

He takes the initiative, asks her to help meet his needs, engages her in conversation by creating an air of mystery, confronts her on her lifestyle, corrects her doctrine and reveals his true identity. The results are transformed lives and an evangelized village.

How do the disciples respond? With joy? No. First they react with unexpressed confusion (v27) and then with distraction (v31). This gives Jesus the perfect teaching opportunity. Having healed Sam's hurting heart, he now proceeds to pry open the disciples' prejudiced pulmonary pumps. His disciples are mystified about something that couldn't be clearer to Jesus. He is a reaper and so are his disciples. The problem is not that they don't understand this principle (they knew they'd been called to be fishers of men), but they hadn't grasped *what this meant in practice*. In the real world this involved meeting, talking to, interacting with, feeling for and helping people who were *different*. This principle applies to us twenty-first century people just as much. We are missional people sent by the Spirit into a mission field prepared for us by God. Jesus shows us what this looks like—getting involved in other people's mess just like Jesus got involved with ours (and still does, by the way).

Confused Eyes

Reading an article about Brian McLaren recently in *Christianity Today*, I was challenged by a comment he made to the effect that the Christian church tends to be more about self-preservation than outreach. I was reminded of a conversation I had two years ago with a lecturer in missiology (the theology of missions). I wanted to talk to him because I was very impressed with his lectures. He had fleshed out for me the theology behind mission. As an evangelist of many seasons, I realized I had been missing some Biblical perspective on this. In terms of method I was well-equipped, but in terms of theology I was shallow. After his lectures I felt my heart more inspired about mission than for many a year.[1] The conversation I had with him went something like this:

> "The churches I am involved with have come to a virtual standstill in terms of mission. What do you suggest I do?"
> "Tell me more about the background to the current situation."
> "We have been a rapidly growing movement of churches with a radical commitment to national and international church planting for many years."
> "So what happened?"
> "We became so focused on mission and growth that this dominated our church life, leading to a neglect of spiritual formation and maturity. We overdosed on growth and became spiritually malnourished."

---

1. I should mention that this man is someone who not only lectures on missions, but is personally involved in mission work. He is at the coalface. There is a big difference between those above ground who talk about mining and those below ground at the coalface (where the coal is being mined) and who come up the mine shaft at the end of an exhausting shift dirty, smelly, tired yet satisfied with their work.

"You're saying your church had an every-member commitment to evangelism and that you over-did it in terms of mission?"

"Yes."

"In all my years of missionary work I have never come across
a church like that."

I sat in stunned silence for a moment. Surely the recent challenges in our family of churches had been paralleled by something
in this lecturer's experience. Not a bit of it. He had never heard of or
seen a church movement that really believed as a movement and as
an every-member conviction that the fields were ripe for harvest to
the extent of overdoing the commitment to the mission. He never
answered my original question. I didn't press him.

Visionary Eyes

I know there must be others in history that have made the same
mistakes my fellowship and I have, and there were many factors that
contributed to some of the challenges in our family of churches. But
the fact remains that we had a good grasp on this point of Jesus in
John chapter 4—the fields are ripe for harvest. It is true that some
are gifted in evangelism (Ephesians 4:11), but all disciples are capable of evangelism and are called to it (Matthew 5:13–16) in one form
or another. The call to touch hearts with the gospel is one we heed-
ed eagerly. Whether the hearts were Asian, African, European,
American or whatever, we opened our lives, hearts and homes to
them. I truly believe that if aliens from Alpha Centauri had landed,
we'd have been happy to share the gospel with and baptize them.

Now if you are reading this book from a church background that
doesn't match mine (or from no church background at all), I crave
your indulgence on this point. It's just that it burns within me that
we not eject baby and bathwater. While it is true that our overdos-
ing on the methods and practice of mission has caused many to need
healing and remedial care (and I include myself in this), it is never-
theless the case that the fields *remain* ripe for harvest, and the joy of

the sower and the reaper can be shared *even now*.

Jesus was hungry, thirsty, hot and tired. Yet he kept his eyes open to the pain of another. The suffering of the world is all around us. Perhaps we see too much of it. The flood is so intense (TV, radio, Internet) that we suffer sensory overload and find it almost impossible to feel the pity and extend the mercy we once did. Where are you with this right now? May I offer the advice that we should pray for compassion?

I had not been feeling good about the lack of sympathy I felt for people in pain, so I started praying for God to work on my heart through whatever means he thought fit. Just this week I was walking home at five o'clock in the afternoon and got caught up in a fight between three men. Two men attacked the third, yelling, screaming and throwing rocks at him. I was behind the man being attacked (Mohammed) and ducked as the lumps of rock were thrown our way. He got one in the head. Blood poured everywhere. His assailants ran off and I offered him my handkerchief to staunch the flow of blood while I called the ambulance and police. He was taken to a hospital, and I feel sure he will be fine physically, but emotionally? Spiritually?

After it was all over, I sat on a low wall nearby trying to take it all in. My handkerchief was soaked in his blood. I took it home and rinsed it again and again in the kitchen sink. The sight of the blood sickened me, and I've found it difficult to get it out of my mind ever since.

Soon after this, one of my neighbors was assaulted by her partner and came to us for comfort and advice. Her trembling, terrified face touched my heart. Like Sam, she needed the healing words of Jesus. Like the royal official she needed a miracle. But above all, this woman and Mohammed needed to know they are not beyond the pale, that they matter to Jesus, that his compassion extends to them. How will they know? How will the people in your office know? How will your family, your neighbors, your friends know? Only if we allow their stories to touch our hearts and awaken the compassion within. Only if we believe the fields are ripe for harvest. Only if we open our eyes.

Jesus was an eye-opener. Let's be the same.

Questions for Reflection

1. Who do you know who is like Sam?
2. Is there a way you can show them you care?
3. When will you talk to them?

Prayer

Father, thanks that your love knew no barrier to loving me. Help me today to love others like you've loved me. Bring to my mind and heart those whose lives and hearts I can touch. Open my eyes to see them as you do. Give me faith for the plentiful harvest. Send me out into that harvest field with love and faith. Here am I, send me. In Jesus' name, Amen.

5

R-E-S-P-E-C-T

John Chapter 5

It seems Jesus loved asking awkward questions.[1] Do you like being interviewed? I don't. I once had an ambition to be an opera singer and went to many auditions. Some went better than others, but all left me in need of a lie-down in a dark room! By the same token, I hate asking people questions. I feel I am being intrusive. It is not uncommon for me to put off conversations with people or phone calls until I've prayed for the strength to be able to ask and be asked questions without developing a nervous tic.

My friend Chris and I discussed the issue of conflict recently. I shared with him my difficulty in raising issues with people. He looked at me and said, "I don't have any problem with that whatso-ever." I thought he was joking for a moment, but then I realized he was serious. I cannot relate! However, I am glad that someone more like Jesus in this area can show me the way.

Jesus did not allow fear of conflict to stop him. Of course he only caused conflict or engaged in conflict when it was necessary to help someone. He wasn't interested in conflict for its own sake. After all, he taught his followers to be peacemakers (Matthew 5:9). Jesus was no bull in a china shop looking for a smashing time. He spoke up when it would bring healing and growth, and this passage shows Jesus at his question-asking best. Before we look at the question he asked, let us consider why he chose this man in the first place.

---

1. Conrad Gempf has written an insightful book on this theme: *Jesus Asked*, (Grand Rapids: Zondervan, 2003).

Why Me?

Have you ever wondered why Jesus chose to speak to this man? I mean, there were "a great number" of needy people at the pool (v3). We can only speculate, but I sense it may have been because this man was in a more desperate situation than anyone else. Today we take it for granted in the West that people with physical or mental challenges are helped and honored. The Special Olympics and the Paralympics are broadcast on TV. A British Paralympian who had already received an MBE and an OBE was made a Dame this year.[2] She deservedly received huge publicity.

Back in Jesus' day things were different. This man's only option for movement was for people to carry him (like the paralytic in Mark 2:3) or if he dragged himself. His hands were likely swathed with rags to help with the friction, but even then the skin would be calloused, scarred, brittle and often bloody. He may well not have had control over his bowels and bladder. If that was true, the stench would have been unbearable—especially in the warm climate of the Middle East. The assumption was that illness was a result of sin (John 9:1–2), so he was unclean and ostracized. Some people speculate that the reason Jesus went back to him and said, "Stop sinning or something worse may happen to you" (v14) may have been because his disability was the result of an accident caused by sin. Perhaps he was a roofer, got drunk one day, fell from a roof while repairing it and ended up paralyzed. In any case, he'd been there thirty-eight years looking and smelling helpless and repulsive.

And yet Jesus is drawn to him as a bee to honey.

Isn't this one of the most amazing things about Jesus? He is attracted like a magnet to the very people I would run from (think also about the demoniac in Mark 5:1–5). What does this tell us about Jesus and God? It tells us no one is so repulsive to him that he will not involve himself in his or her problems (reflect on the situation of the lost son in Luke 15:11–24). I am consistently disappointed in myself that I'm drawn to some people and not to others. No doubt Jesus would have enjoyed being around people like me, but

---

2. Dame Tanni Grey-Thompson won sixteen medals, including eleven gold. She was awarded the MBE (Member of the Order of the British Empire) and the OBE (Order of the British Empire) before receiving the higher title of "Dame" this year.

he would have also loved to talk to people completely different from me. There should be no competition in our lives as to who gets loved. Parents must love all their children equally. Office workers must love the janitor and the boss. Teachers must love the student and the principal. This is hard.

R-E-S-P-E-C-T

If I may boast about my wife a little—this is an area in which she excels and sets a tremendous example. She returned to practice medicine after a long break in which she served on the full-time church staff. It would be fair to say she had some insecurity about how to conduct herself at work as a Christian having been out of the secular workforce for sixteen years. Should she deliberately drop "church" into conversations? Might some religious language help? Perhaps inviting colleagues to church meetings would make things clear.

She made a decision to pray and just be her (Christian) self. Everyone at work soon came to know she was a Christian—simply because she treated *everyone* with respect. Where nurses, doctors, anesthetists, pharmacists, physiotherapists, occupational therapists, radiologists, porters, patients, administrators and managers had conflicts, she had friendships. Several people said to her things such as, "You're friendly to *everyone!*" as if this was really weird—which in the work culture it was. You will not be surprised when I tell you a number of her colleagues invited themselves to church.

It is amazing how true Christian character shines out. Often I feel we struggle with the issue of "evangelism" when we should be struggling with the issue of "beatitudenism"—growing in the characteristics of Kingdom people as laid out in Matthew 5:1–12. Growing in the latter will give success to the former. Can you show greater respect to some people at work, in your family or your neighborhood?

Designer Label

The big deal is showing respect to all people. If people are made in God's image (Genesis 1:26–27) then we are duty-bound to respect everyone. If we do not value the creation, we do not respect the Creator. "Yes, yes," I hear you say, "I agree with this, so what's your point?" My point is this:

> Jesus demonstrated that all people were valuable to God by
> *deliberately* going out of his way
> to *involve* himself in the lives of those people in society
> who were *not* considered to be valuable.

I am frightened by this realization. It occurs to me that as a Christian I am in danger of exchanging one set of prejudices for another. I identify with Philip Yancey's observation in his tremendous book *Soul Survivor*. He writes about how he had

> ...substituted a new kind of fundamentalism for the old, one born of snobbery rather than ignorance. How blithely I point out the sins and failures of my childhood churches, and how rarely I dwell on the goodness I also found there. I used to look down on blacks; now I look down on racists. I used to avoid the rich; now I avoid the poor."[3]

How easy it is to label people. *Racist, Pedophile, Homosexual.* The label gives us an excuse to keep our distance. I will never forget the first time I discussed homosexuality with another disciple. His face contorted horribly. I thought he was having a spasm. He could barely spit out the words of derision and hatred as he left me in no doubt about what he thought their fate should be. If he had his wish they would all be rounded up and shot at dawn.

How about this thought? If Jesus were around today, you would be just as likely to find him having lunch with a racist bigot as an evangelical believer. Jesus grasped something we tend to forget—people are people, not labels. One of the best-known passages that condemns homosexuality (1 Corinthians 6:9–10) also lists other sins such as slander, drunkenness and greed. There doesn't appear to be

---

3. Philip Yancey, *Soul Survivor* (New York: Hodder and Stoughton, 2003), 102.

any distinction between the seriousness of these sins in that passage. Any of them will keep the unrepentant out of the Kingdom of God. But do we hear sermons as powerful in the condemnation of greed as that of homosexuality? Let's face it, are church members (or people who visit the church, for that matter) more likely to be tempted to commit homosexual acts or greedy acts? Sure, the Bible teaches that homosexual practices are sin, but what about its teaching on greed? Consider the following verses:

I was enraged by his sinful greed;
    I punished him, and hid my face in anger,
    yet he kept on in his willful ways. (Isaiah 57:17)

Therefore I will give their wives to other men
    and their fields to new owners.
From the least to the greatest,
    all are greedy for gain;
prophets and priests alike,
    all practice deceit. (Jeremiah 8:10)

My people come to you, as they usually do, and sit before you to listen to your words, but they do not put them into practice. With their mouths they express devotion, but their hearts are greedy for unjust gain. (Ezekiel 33:31)

"Woe to you, teachers of the law and Pharisees, you hypocrites! You clean the outside of the cup and dish, but inside they are full of greed and self-indulgence." (Matthew 23:25)

"For from within, out of men's hearts, come evil thoughts, sexual immorality, theft, murder, adultery, greed, malice, deceit, lewdness, envy, slander, arrogance and folly. All these evils come from inside and make a man 'unclean.'" (Mark 7:21)

"Watch out! Be on your guard against all kinds of greed; a man's life does not consist in the abundance of his possessions." (Luke 12:15)

> But now I am writing you that you must not associate with anyone who calls himself a brother but is sexually immoral or greedy, an idolater or a slanderer, a drunkard or a swindler. With such a man do not even eat. (1 Corinthians 5:11)

> But among you there must not be even a hint of sexual immorality, or of any kind of impurity, or of greed, because these are improper for God's holy people. ...For of this you can be sure: No immoral, impure or greedy person—such a man is an idolater—has any inheritance in the kingdom of Christ and of God. (Ephesians 5:3, 5)

> Put to death, therefore, whatever belongs to your earthly nature: sexual immorality, impurity, lust, evil desires and greed, which is idolatry. (Colossians 3:5)

So the question is this: are you more uncomfortable around a homosexual or a greedy person? I will be honest. I find conversations with homosexuals much more challenging than those with greedy people. I am ashamed of this and I know it is not Christlike. Pray for me as I try to love all people equally. Pray for me as I try to imitate Jesus. Pray for me that the Spirit of Christ will transform me not just in actions, but, much more importantly, in my heart.

My point, as I hope is clear, is not about homosexuality or greed but about examining our assumptions and preconceptions. I confess I am a prejudiced, self-righteous person—but I suspect I am not alone. To whom do you show prejudice? We all like to think we don't have any prejudices, but try this exercise. Take a look at your circle of friends. Then take a look at your neighborhood and your workplace. What kind of person is represented in your environment, but not in attendance at your birthday party? We are commanded by God to love *all* his children. As far as he is concerned my label is not "white middle-class male" but "made in his image."

Get to the Question

I apologize if I have strayed a little from the significance of the miraculous healing in this chapter, but I feel that one of the greatest lessons we can take from this passage is the issue of respect. This even helps explain the reason for Jesus' curious question.

How many different explanations have you heard as to why Jesus asked the question "Do you want to get well?" (v6). What a strange question. Surely it was obvious he wanted to get well. Surely Jesus, knowing all things (16:30, 21:17) and being able to determine people's thoughts (Mark 2:8, Luke 6:8), must have known the man wanted to get well. He didn't need to ask the question. So why did he? I think there are several possible explanations, but here is mine:

> Jesus asked the question because he wanted to show the man respect.

What do I mean? Well, don't you hate it when someone tells you what you need before you've had a chance to explain yourself? Proverbs 18:13 says, "He who answers before listening—that is his folly and his shame." I get this from telesales people (sorry telesales operatives—this is nothing personal; I am sure there are some wonderful telesales people out there). It is just that I seem to get called by all the ones who "know" I need a new mobile phone or a "free" holiday (not including flights, taxes and catering) and won't take "No" for an answer.

When people ignore your response, it reveals they don't *really* care about you. Someone who really cares takes the time to step into your situation, your pain, your confusion. Jesus knew what this man wanted. He knew what this man needed. He knew the problems. Jesus showed the man ultimate respect by acknowledging he had choices. He had the choice to remain as he was. He had the choice to ask for or at least accept help from Jesus. Jesus didn't force his solution onto this man—needy as he was. Aid workers will tell you that unless you respect the local people, all the food supplies, medical assistance and housing projects will become sources of resentment, even though the community is desperate for them.

One last thing remains. I am conflicted as I reflect on the fact that we have barely gotten wet in John chapter 5. We have not even so much as glanced at verses sixteen to forty-seven. I shall have to leave those verses in your hands, dear reader. There is one thing I would like to mention, however. The rest of the chapter is largely a defense of Jesus' authority. Set here right after this amazing encounter between the man by the pool and Jesus, it provides a window into the heart of God. As Jesus says in verse nineteen, "...the Son can do nothing by himself; he can do only what he sees his Father doing, because whatever the Father does the Son also does." The loving, respectful treatment of the invalid by Jesus is *exactly* the treatment God wanted shown the man. This is testimony to the compassionate heart of God and is a reminder that if we want to know the nature of God, we must look deep into the actions of Jesus. There we will find the motives of the Creator and learn of his compassion for all of us.

So as you have read John chapter 5 and the chapter above, has your conscience been stirred? Is there someone you struggle to respect at work or at church? Can you pray and find it within the love of God to grow the patience and heart to love a "difficult to love" person?

Questions for Reflection

1. Is there someone you struggle to respect as a child of God, someone at the "poolside" waiting for you? Can you involve yourself with them in a way that demonstrates you do respect them in the same way God does?

2. Will you make a commitment to acknowledging that people have choices before you give them the benefit of your advice? The next time you are tempted to give advice that someone "obviously" needs, will you show respect by first asking whether they want your wisdom?

3. In what way has God spoken to you in this chapter? What might he be whispering in your ear? If you have heard his voice, do not delay. Act on it today.

Prayer

Father, your respect for your creation amazes me. Your patience with the human race inspires me. Grant me a heart to respect every man and woman—all those made in your image no matter what race or religion they embrace. Help me to see people as people, not as labels. Wipe the blindness of prejudice away from my eyes, and give me the love of Jesus for all around me. In Jesus' name, Amen.

6

Super-Sandwich

John Chapter 6

When I was a kid, my mother sent me off on school trips with a hearty packed lunch. Inside were enormous multi-layered sandwiches. Between the slices of homemade bread there was ham or cheese, perhaps fish paste or something called "sandwich spread," and several pieces of salad (lettuce, tomato and cucumber with the occasional radish, spring onion or slice of beetroot). At some point on the trip, lunch was eaten and I played the game of try-to-take-a-bite-of-my-sandwich-without-something-sliding-out-and-landing-on-the-floor. My fellow pupils found this more amusing than I did.

In chapter 6, John packs a lot of stuff together to make one enormous, nutritious spiritual sandwich. This is a monster of a chapter! Not ugly, just huge. It has several layers and many ingredients.

The Big Picnic

Jesus loved feasts. His first sign was at a wedding feast (John 2), and his fifth sign was this outdoor picnic. Mind you, things didn't look too promising at the start. The thousands had not packed their lunch boxes with the same diligence as my mother. Only one mum had provided her son with the loaves and fish that would get him through the trip. Can't you see the glint in Jesus' eye as he asks the question, "Where shall we buy bread for all these people?" I can hear him chuckle quietly as he hears Andrew comment on the lack of resources, "…how far will these go among so many?"

There is humor in this passage—although things get deadly serious pretty quickly. It seems to me Jesus is consciously comparing and contrasting himself with the three greatest miracle-workers of Old Testament times: Moses, Elijah and Elisha. This feeding from little or nothing recapitulates the feeding of the Israelites in the desert (Exodus 16), the feeding of the widow and her son (1 Kings17:7–16) and the feeding of the 100 men (2 Kings 4:42–44).

Here we see John making the point that Jesus was not just another Moses, Elijah or Elisha (impressive though that might be). Jesus will eclipse their achievements. This is emphasized by the abundance of leftovers. Excess manna went rotten (Exodus 16:20), the oil and flour fed only one family (1 Kings 17:15–16) and in 2 Kings 4 we are told there was "some" left over (v44). Here, however, there are twelve baskets of scraps. Again, in the incident that follows (John 6:16–21), Jesus *walks* on water while Moses, Elijah and Elisha only *parted* the waters (Exodus 14:21–22, 2 Kings 2:8–14).

Exceeding Expectations

In most situations it is really satisfying when our expectations are surpassed. As I write this, the temperature in London is 34 Celsius (93 Fahrenheit)—in the shade. That is hotter than the south of Spain. Tomorrow the forecast is to be even hotter. Some of you who live abroad think of London as the land of perpetual cloud and drizzle and would be pleasantly surprised to be here at the moment. This sunshine is great, although it does bring its own problems. We are also in the middle of a drought. There is less water available in the Southeast of England per capita than in Egypt, Morocco or Kenya. So although the weather has exceeded our expectations, there is another side.

The crowd is happy for Jesus to be the Prophet and would like him to be their king (vv14–15). He has in many ways exceeded their expectations. But they are *not* ready to allow him to redefine their view of what it means to please God (vv28–29, 41, 52, 60–61, 66). They are not ready for the full reality of what it means for him to be Prophet and king.

Similarly, the disciples are happy to be his sign-observing side-kicks, but are terrified when Jesus turns up alongside their boat strolling on the water (v19). Some of his disciples (although not the Twelve) decided to turn away (v66). The decision the deserters made points to a crucial principle for all who want to follow Jesus. One question must be resolved by everyone who decides to become a disciple. Not only must they resolve it at the point of their initial decision, but they must continue to commit themselves to this same principle. The question is this:

Are you ready to let Jesus define what it means to follow him?

And the follow-up question is similar,

Are you ready to change your beliefs and lifestyle accordingly whatever the consequences?

I dare say most of us are in the "Yes" camp on these questions; living up to this is harder than it sounds.

The influence of the world is strong. Society values tolerance so highly that this often eclipses truth. It is no longer acceptable to have firm views on the sanctity of life (abortion, euthanasia, embryo research, etc.). One is labeled a bigot for holding that homosexuality and same-sex marriages are sin. Yet would not Jesus be labeled intolerant today—despite his evident compassion for the marginalized and oppressed of the world? He did not condemn people, but he called sin, sin (John 8:11) and expected repentance (Luke 13:1–9, 19:1–10).

This same attitude of tolerance is also often abroad in the religious world. There is an entirely understandable desire to accept all who make any profession of Christian faith without examining their doctrines or lifestyles. Yet is this how Jesus operated? He challenged the religious establishment of his day (Matthew 23:1–39, John 2:12–25, 3:1–15) and condemned false teaching (Matthew 23:15,

Mark 12:24). He made it clear that there would be people who walked, talked and looked like his followers and yet who, in reality, had nothing to do with him (Matthew 7:15–23).

The Challenge of Change

What does this mean for a follower of Jesus? It means we must be open to being taught new doctrines and refining old ones. It means we must be open to any challenge to our lifestyle that can be backed by Scripture. Here is a question for those of us who follow Jesus Christ:

> *When was the last time you changed a belief because the Bible made it clear you had been wrong?*

Here is another one:

> *When was the last time you changed something in your lifestyle because the Bible made it clear you had been wrong?*

Some might say that I am in danger of motivating by fear. Well, for one thing there is nothing wrong with making changes when motivated by the right kind of fear (Philippians 2:12). I started wearing a bike helmet a few years ago even though I grew up not wearing one and hate wearing the thing. I am genuinely and healthily afraid of being knocked off my bike (and I have been).

In addition there is great joy in repenting, maturing and being transformed into the likeness of Christ. Such joys are worth the pain of change and even the feeling of fear (Acts 3:19). Repentance is a joy not a drudge. Any of us who have confessed a sin have experienced the joy of renewed closeness to God and clarity of conscience. Maturing in Christ is not easy, but it is worth it. God is currently in the process of training me to be more self-disciplined and humble. I would be a liar if I said this was fun, but I am persuaded that the long-term blessings outweigh the short-term struggles (at least, I *hope* it is short-term!).

In recent times my wife and I have become increasingly concerned about our lack of responsible stewardship of God's creation. This is too big an issue to engage in detail here, but suffice to say we have changed how we bank, eat, recycle, exercise and shop as a result of our changed Biblical convictions. Some of these changes have been easy; others have been hard. We are a little worse off financially, but much better off spiritually. I am confident we now have a lifestyle that more accurately reflects a Christlike perspective on creation and the environment. I doubt that is the end of the matter, and we will continue to learn more, but at least we've made a step.

Gifts, Givers and Special Occasions

Have you ever seen a parent rapturous over a gift from their small child? I do not know how many leather (or fake leather) bookmarks I gave my mother each time I went on holiday, but there must have been enough to equip a library full of books. As I was growing up, the only present I gave her every year was a walnut whip. This confectionary concoction was a conico/pyramidic swirl of chocolate topped by a small piece of walnut. My father was given an annual birthday Aero Bar—basically chocolate with tiny air holes in it. They never complained. At least, not to my knowledge. Gifts of insignificant monetary worth have great value when they signify the outer limits of a person's giving ability (Luke 21:1–4).

One of the most moving sights in my life was at our wedding reception. My wife's father gave his father-of-the-bride speech. He pulled out an old piece of paper that had clearly been carefully preserved for many years. It was a card from my wife to her father written when she was a small girl. On it she had drawn a simple picture and told her dad how much she loved him. As my father-in-law read the note, we all cried. He sat down, and you could have heard a pin drop. The "insignificant" piece of paper was transformed by the special nature of their relationship and the significance of the occasion.

Rarely does the value of the gift match the significance of the occasion and the status of the giver. In order to buy my wife an engagement ring, I sold my French horn. It was the only thing of value I possessed (apart from my kidneys, but selling them would have been illegal). Was there any debate in my mind as to whether it was worth it? No way! It was a sacrifice willingly made by a person who knew he was on to a good thing. The value of the French horn matched the monetary value of the ring, but didn't come close to matching the significance of the ring.

A few years ago I turned forty (I know it is hard to believe, but I *am* that old). I was asked by several people what I wanted for my birthday. Several of my friends made suggestions: a Harley, a hair transplant, a Zimmer frame, shares in Saga, a vat of prune juice. I have such nice friends. Anyway, I asked for gifts that were personal rather than monetary. My daughter (who was twelve at the time) excelled herself and wrote me a poem. It was called, "I Am Glad U R My Dad!" and went like this:

It was on the 25th of May,
A very, very special day,
Another human given life,
Which came from your beloved wife.
Lydia was her name,
Having fun was her game,
And into the world I came,
And I am glad u r my dad.

You cared for me and changed my nappy,
And cuddled me when I was sad or happy.
As I aged you watched me grow,
From my head down to my toes.
You took me places I'd never seen,
And held me close after a scary dream.
You and me we are a team,
And I am glad u r my dad.

Now I've aged and so have you,
12 candles on my cake I blew,
and I'm big and at high school,
having fun and breaking rules.

And when at school I've had a bad day,
I come home and you're there always.
Everything will be okay,
Coz I am glad u r my dad.

Thank you for always being there,
And showing me you really care.
You always help me when I get stuck,
And comfort me when I have bad luck.
When I'm angry you make me smile,
And you're there to show me life's worthwhile.
When you're around I'm never sad,
Coz I am glad u r my dad.

And now it is that time of year,
When we get together with friends and peers,
To celebrate your 40th birthday.
And I'd just like to say,
You are the best dad around,
And when I hug you I just can't frown
There is just one more thing I'd love to add …

I am glad U R my Dad!

I was given many special gifts that day, but none brought me as close to tears as this one. My special one and only daughter had created something unique with great effort and thought, and had given it to me on one of the most significant days of my life. The significance of the gift matched the significance of the giver and the significance of the occasion. I treasure this poem. Even typing it into this chapter brought me to the verge of tears. Lydia is out of the house at the moment, but when she comes home I want to give her a big hug and tell her again how much I love her. Who knows, this poem may well resurface at Lydia's wedding reception when that day comes (don't tell her I said that)!

In this short chapter, I cannot possibly do justice to the depth and majesty of the teaching contained in John 6:25–71. I toyed with what to do with the issues raised in this passage for some considerable time. In the end, rather than do it an injustice I decided to do two things.

First, I'd like to ask you to reflect on what I have written above and to think about the significance of bringing together gift, giver and special occasion. Second, I'd like to ask you to reflect on the fact that it was only the Twelve that even began to grasp the significance of the bringing together of *gift* (Jesus as the bread of life, as the giver of eternal life, as one greater than Moses, as the gift of God—John 6:27, 2 Corinthians 9:15), the *giver* (God as giver of life, his Word and the Word made flesh—John 1:1, 14; 3:16-21; 6:29, 32) and the *special occasion* (Passover—John 6:4). Even the Twelve caught only the fringe of what this was about, but it was enough for them to hang on and not turn back like so many others.

Have you felt like giving up recently? Are you more comfortable in the company of "grumblers" than "stayers"? Remember that the grumblers here (vv41, 43, 52, 61) are standing in the tradition of the desert grumblers of Moses' day (Exodus 15:24, 16:2–12, 17:3). Things didn't go too well for them (no entry to the promised land, death in the desert, etc.). What separated the Twelve from the rest? Intelligence? Theological education? Social standing? Ownership of a special "Religious Insight Gene"? I don't think so. What made them stand out was that they were prepared to trust the Lord that they knew for the things they didn't yet understand. What a good model for us.

In summary, we see this truth laid out in chapter 6—when Jesus demands something unreasonable, asks you to believe something unbelievable, requests you take on board a conviction that seems impossible, think hard before dropping the baton or looking for an easier way.

Questions for Reflection

1. Have you become too comfortable in your expectations of what Jesus can do in you and through you? Is it time to pray for him to do something miraculous around you or in you? Buckle up. It could be a bumpy ride!

2. When was the last time you thanked God for his indescribable generosity, his incredible gifts and his promise of the life to come? Is there some way you could imitate this generosity in the life of someone around you? What will you do for whom and when?

3. Have you been tempted to give up following Jesus? Why? When the end of your life comes, do you want to be mad at Jesus or glad you persevered?

Prayer

Father, thank you that your Son is so real yet so different. Help me to value his demands to be different and not to desire a comfortable life that just fits in with the world. Give me strength to persevere because there are times I just want to give up. I want to be like the Twelve. Give me a glimpse of the excitement of a life lived on the edge and the trust in you that I can make it. In the name of the Bread of Life, Jesus my Lord, Amen.

7

Confusion and Refreshment

John Chapter 7

I have a friend called Tim. Tim confuses me. I consider this to be one of the greatest blessings in my life.

You may need to read that sentence again. Perhaps it didn't say what you expected. After all, we don't enjoy being confused. I have known Tim for over twenty years. We are good friends, have been through thick and thin times, and talked about everything and anything to do with life and faith. You would think we'd understand each other by now. He still confuses me—and that's a good thing! You see, I need people in my life who think so differently from me that my basic assumptions are challenged. Tim brings some holy confusion to my thinking—and long may he do so.

Who confuses you? No, not your income tax form or quantum mechanics lecturer or pension advisor. I mean, who is disturbing your thinking about life and faith? I am tempted not to call Tim sometimes even though he is a godly man and a good friend. I'm afraid he might challenge my precious certainties. But why am I afraid? Is it because I might be wrong? The older I get, the more I realize how many of my assumptions are just plain incorrect.

Why are you reading this book? I guess you are following, or want to follow, Jesus Christ. Did you realize that he wants to confuse you? "No, no," you say, "Jesus is supposed to comfort me, remove uncertainty, provide direction, guarantee my destiny!" This is true. But before we can be comforted, guided and reassured, we must have our assumptions challenged. This is what Jesus did to every person around him. He challenges us as we consider following him, and he continues to challenge us throughout our lives. Confusion is one of Jesus' methods of promoting spiritual growth and maturity in us. That sounds a bit weird, but let us examine this principle more closely.

Jesus the Confuser

He is misunderstood by his mother (2:4), his brothers (7:6–8), Nicodemus (3:1–10), the crowds (7:12, 20, 40–44), the temple guards (7:45–49), his own disciples (4:31–34), the Pharisees (7:45–52) and the Jews as a whole (6:41–42, 7:15, 35–36). Confusion reigns in this chapter. Jesus is stirring things up. He seems to be making life harder for himself than it has to be. Why?

Because the people around him have expectations of him that are not right.

Unless he says and does things that look weird to those around him, he will never get them to see things the way he does. His brothers assume he wants to be a "public figure" (v4). Perhaps they have the impression Jesus wants to be famous. "If you want to get your message across, go and get on one of those reality TV shows," they could have said. We know that many were hoping for a kingly David-like Messiah who would boot out the Romans (6:15). Some were looking for food without commitment (6:53, 66).

We have the same challenge today. We all want to construct a Jesus according to our own preferences. "Oh no, not me," you may say. "I believe in the Jesus of the Bible." Well let me ask you this.

When was the last time Jesus confused you?

If we are not confused (at least by something) then we are in danger of closing our minds to learning, growing and maturing. When I am being honest, I can admit to many things in my life that confuse me. Why do I still struggle with anxiety and lack of discipline after twenty years as a disciple? Why was my mother severely disabled all through my childhood? Why don't my kids love classical music the way I do (ouch, that hurts!)? Why does it seem that so many of the sacrifices I make for God are not rewarded in the here-and-now? Why does God allow firestorms in his church and my life—*and why do they come when I'm not ready for them?!*

Take a minute and write down some of the things that you are confused about. Making a list might help you identify the things you feel anxious or angry about. Do not be afraid to be honest with God. Job was, and although God was firm with him, he also brought him to a place of comfort and understanding (Job 30:20–22, 38:1–3, 42:12–17).

Father, I'm confused about:

_____

_____

_____

_____

_____

_____

Now that we have reflected on our present confusions, let's go back and look at some of the issues confusing the people around Jesus.

Harvest Festival

The Feast of Tabernacles (v2) was held in September/October each year and was the last of the yearly cycle of festivals. It was a bit like our "harvest festival" or even Thanksgiving in the U.S. It was the most popular of all the festivals. It came to be called simply "The Feast" and lasted seven days with an eighth day of special celebrations. On that last and greatest day of the feast, Jesus makes quite an amazing claim: "'If anyone is thirsty, let him come to me and drink. Whoever believes in me, as the Scripture has said, streams of living water will flow from within him.' By this he meant the Spirit, whom those who believed in him were later to receive. Up to that time the Spirit had not been given, since Jesus had not yet been glorified" (vv37–39).

His hearers would doubtless have thought of several Old Testament passages including Isaiah 12:3 and 58:11. Isaiah 12:3 can be seen as dealing with personal salvation: "With joy you will draw water from the wells of salvation." But the passage in Isaiah 58:11 makes it clear that those who receive refreshment will be able to refresh others. A garden and a never-failing stream are sure to attract others, sustain others and provide a home for many:

> "The LORD will guide you always;
>   he will satisfy your needs in a sun-scorched land
>   and will strengthen your frame.
> You will be like a well-watered garden,
>   like a spring whose waters never fail."

So what Jesus is saying is this: as the one with authority to send the Spirit streaming into "those who believed in him" (v39), he is providing access to salvation that does not stop with the individual recipient. The stream will never fail to provide blessings to others, as well as the possessor of the Spirit. For centuries priests had poured out water at the height of the Feast of Tabernacles symbolizing this future pouring out of God's favor. Now Jesus stands there and claims the symbolism as a reality fulfilled in himself.

All Christians are people who have received this outpouring of the Spirit and are supposed to be a channel for others to receive this blessing. Are you confused about this blessing and this responsibility? Do you sense God's Spirit pouring out of you? Have people noticed the fountain of faith cascading from your heart into the world around you? Is the carpet soggy around your chair at work? Are your children getting damp? Does your spouse see you in full-flood? Are your housemates and neighbors swimming in the pool created by your devotion to Christ? Perhaps it is time to stop holding back the dam, to open the floodgates, and dismantle the dyke.

Getting the Point

Jesus' hearers get into complex debates in chapter 7. They discuss his origins (v27), his miracle credentials (v31), his destination (v35), his identity (vv40–41) and his birthplace (v42).

But they miss the point entirely!

The point was to believe in Jesus, receive the Spirit, experience transformation (3:3–5) and bless others.

Do we get the point? It is tempting to discuss, debate and spend much time and energy over disputable matters when the real issue is enjoying the life-changing presence of the Spirit and expressing this in love for others. What are you focused on today? Let it be believing, being filled, living in obedience to Jesus (8:31–32), enjoying the on-going Christ-focused transformation that is available and spilling over to bless those around us with the joy that comes with the Holy Spirit.

Is Jesus confusing you? In your life do you have a "Tim" who causes some Christian confusion? Call him (or her) today. Do not stay away from sources of Christian confusion (the Scriptures and godly friends, mostly). Instead embrace them and cling to Jesus who will make all things clear in his own time and way. We all have John chapter 7 periods in our lives, but if we stay close to the Lord, we will be around to experience the Acts 2 moments as well. In that chapter we see the fruition of what Jesus talked about in this passage.

Questions for Reflection

1. What confuses you most about the Christian life?
2. Who confuses you most in a helpful way about what you believe and how you live?
3. What can you do to grow in your understanding of what God is teaching you in the areas that confuse you most right now?

Prayer

Father of confusion and clarity, thank you for disturbing my world. Thank you for making me think about what is and is not important. Help me recognize my assumptions and let your Holy Spirit challenge them. Sometimes Jesus confuses me, and I do not know what he means or where he's taking me. Give me strength to get through my John 7 questions so that I can experience the Acts 2 answers. Help me trust him for direction and listen to him for understanding, never giving up on him. In Jesus' name, Amen.

8

Questions, Questions, Questions

John Chapter 8

What is your number one question for God? I mean, when you die and re-awake in heaven, what is the first thing you will ask the Lord? "What was Jesus writing on the ground in John 8:6?" "Who wrote Hebrews?" Or maybe a deeper, more troubling question: "Why did my young cousin have to die a violent death?" What about you? Do you have a question? Take a moment to think about this and then write it down.

My Lord, what I really want to know is

_____

_____

_____

_____

You may or may not get your question answered this side of glory. As we travel through life asking questions, it becomes clear that some are considered legitimate by God and some are not. Perhaps it is not the specific questions that are the issue, but the spirit in which they are asked. Job asks "Why?!" questions of God and in return is challenged with, "Brace yourself like a man; I will question you and you shall answer me" (Job 38:3). God answered Job's questions with questions of his own. On the other hand, God answers Gideon's "Why?" and "How?" questions patiently (Judges 6.13–16). Questions are normal and acceptable to God—if asked in the right spirit.

But there is another side to questions. Not questions *we* ask out of ignorance or curiosity, but questions that others ask of us because of the way we live. Our lives are meant to make people think, to provoke questions. This aspect of questions strikes me in chapter 8 as a remarkable habit of Jesus:

Jesus provoked questions everywhere he went. Do you?

I mean, if we are his disciples, following him, imitating him, walking as he did, then the same thing should be happening to us— shouldn't it? This kind of challenge stops me in my tracks every time. It is sober-thinking time (Romans 12:3). In John 8 Jesus is asked question after question, and constantly challenged on his actions and words. Here are some of the questions and challenges thrown his way:

- "What do you say?" (v5)
- "Your testimony is not valid." (v13)
- "Where is your father?" (v19)
- "Will he kill himself? Is that why he says…?" (v22)
- "Who are you?" (v25)
- "How can you say that we shall be set free?" (v33)
- "Aren't we right in saying…?" (v48)
- "Are you greater than our father Abraham?" (v53)
- "Who do you think you are?" (v53)

The Temperature's Rising

No, I am not referring to a line in the song by The Weather Girls ("It's Raining Men"), but in this chapter we find Jesus under sustained attack and an ever-growing threat of violence (v59). Notice the mood of the crowds (can we leave "of the crowds" out? It's the

Pharisees mostly and not crowds) changing as the chapter goes on. The three key questions for me are the ones in verses 5, 25 and 53. The first, *"What do you say?"* is not innocent because they are trying to trap him (see verse 6), but the question is not threatening in and of itself. There is the possibility of dialogue, of increasing understanding. It is more a question of ideology, doctrine or pastoral practice than it is of identity. The attack on his identity will intensify momentarily.

The second question, *"Who are you?"* is more intrusive. The inquisitors are beginning to reveal the real intentions behind their questions. They are confused, but rather than keeping an open mind and examining Jesus' identity on his own terms (the fulfillment of prophecy and his actions that made clear his identity as Messiah), they want an answer that would not be so disturbing.

The third question, *"Who do you think you are?"* is the most invasive. Jesus' identity and authority are questioned. The questioners are "losing the plot"; they are becoming fuelled by emotion. Anger now dominates, and minds have been closed.

I am sure it is no coincidence that the chapter begins and ends with an attempted stoning. Neither is successful. The context of the earlier stoning (of the woman caught in adultery) is an attempt to trap Jesus (in his words). The context of the second stoning is also an attempt to trap him (this time physically) since the first approach didn't work. The Pharisees seem not to be interested in truth but in self-justification. The woman caught in adultery is not a person to them but an object—a badly-disguised elephant trap.

I suspect the Pharisees were hoping Jesus would pick up a stone and use it against the woman. I imagine one of them approaching Jesus with a particularly holy-looking rock in his hand and asking the question, "Now what do you say, Jesus?" It is at this point that Jesus bends down to write on the ground, leaving the hapless Pharisee with rock-laden hand outstretched and looking gormless. His motives are exposed. He is not interested in justice or mercy, but in pushing Jesus into a corner. Sometimes the best way to respond to an entrapment is by withdrawing.

Are you feeling under fire? Are friends attacking your faith? Do work colleagues try to push you to compromise? How do we handle this? Jesus frequently answered questions with a question of his own (Mark 10:2–3, Luke 20:2–4), but in this chapter he has a quite different approach. Let's look at Jesus and some of the other ways he dealt with question-pressure.

I've Got Witnesses

I am no legal expert (any understanding I have of law comes from John Grisham novels), but I am pretty certain that if you are accused of something, you are in a much better position if you have lots of highly credible witnesses. John brings together an impressive array of witnesses to back up the truthfulness of Jesus' claims.

- John the Baptist—"He came only as a witness to the light" (1:8). See also 1:7–8, 15, 32, 34; 3:32; 5:33.
- Jesus himself (3:11, 13:21, 18:37) as well as his deeds—"The miracles I do in my Father's name speak for me" (10:25). See also 5:36; 8:14, 18; 10:32, 37–38.
- The Father—"My other witness is the Father, who sent me" (8:18). See also the relationship between Jesus and his Father especially in chapters 5–8, 10, 12, 15, 17.
- Moses (5:46) and the Scriptures—"These are the Scriptures that testify about me…" (5:39).
- The Spirit—"When the Counselor comes…the Spirit of truth…he will testify about me" (15:26). See also the in-depth teaching on the witness of the Spirit in chapters 14–16.
- The Disciples—"And you also must testify, for you have been with me from the beginning" (15:27). Look also at the witness they bear to him in chapters 1, 13 and 15.

One of the best ways to answer questions is to appeal to credible authorities. Many people who ask questions are going to be more impressed if your answers have the ring of authority and credibility.

What is the most credible authority to appeal to when we are questioned about our faith? In most cases the best way to answer questions is to talk about your own personal experience. If finding God has secured your destiny, if knowing Christ has brought you peace, if the transforming Spirit has changed your heart, then share about such things.

It is good to learn apologetic arguments (reasons to believe in God, the resurrection, and so on), but the best place to *start* is usually with personal experience.[1] It didn't take me long as a young disciple to learn a few verses to defend the doctrine of baptism for the forgiveness of sins, or the fact that sexual immorality is a sin.

However, most of my neighbors are not impressed by this and will not be persuaded to listen to the gospel by discussing these topics. What the skeptics want to know (especially in this secular/pagan world we live in) is whether your religion is *real*. We are so used to the polished "sincerity" of politicians, the creative persuasion of advertisers, and even the practiced professionalism of preachers that anyone with an authentic story to tell shines out like a maglite torch in a coal cellar.

What do I mean by sharing about our experience? It is easier to explain what I do *not* mean. I am not talking about subjective feelings (although feelings may be part of your story). What I *do* mean are the things that you see, with hindsight, were the ways God led you into a relationship with him and how that relationship has grown since you first met. Not sure how to do that? If you are married, you should hopefully be able to tell people about the history and meaning of your relationship with your wife. I can speak eloquently and at great length about how I met Penny (my wife), what I was thinking when we first got to know each other, how I was feeling before and after we met, and how our friendship has deepened and matured in the twenty-five years we've known each other.

Being single does not mean you are at any disadvantage. We've all had friends (at least, I hope you have!) and to one extent or

---

1. I am a fan of good apologetics like that of Ravi Zacharias, Lee Strobel, John Polkinghorne and my good friend Douglas Jacoby (www.douglasjacoby.com), so please don't misunderstand me here. I'm not against knowing this stuff, just trying to make the point that a good argument will not replace authenticity.

another we can talk about those relationships on a level that is factually accurate and emotionally relevant. Why not share about your relationship with God in a similar way? Try it next time you are asked why you go to church, or why you don't swear, or what motivates you to read your Bible.

Reflecting on this, it occurs to me that I am often afraid of questions. This should not be so. Why should I fear questions? This is an interesting question in itself! I should not fear questions (for they are God-given opportunities to share my faith). I should not fear being asked a question to which I do not know the answer (for there is no one on earth who knows the answer to every question). What I *should* fear is not having something authentic, genuine and real to say about the God I love, the Christ I serve and the Spirit I know.

I guess this comes back to our own personal devotion to God. Is the relationship real, living, growing? If it is, you will naturally have something important to say when you are questioned. If it is not, you have only theories. Yes, our relationship with God must be informed and guided by doctrine, but it must also be true that we do have a *relationship* with God and not just knowledge *about* Him.

Why was Jesus so confident in the face of such persistent, hostile questioning? "Oh, that's easy," we say. "He knew he was the Messiah." I am convinced this was not the reason for his confidence. He did not have a special "no fear" gene. Remember, he was just like us (Hebrews 2:17–18). No, I think he was so confident because *he knew the Father*. When we reel from the impact of hostile questioning, when we lose confidence because we don't know all the answers, we are missing the point. We are to be confident because we know our God. He has made himself known, and we have entered into a living relationship with him.

What an irony to be disciples who feel confident of their salvation (as we should be) and yet unconfident in the face of questions about the faith. We are offered a vision and a hope in 1 John 2:28:

> And now, dear children, continue in him, so that when he appears we may be confident and unashamed before him at his coming.

If we are continuing in him (15:4), walking *in* him and *like* him (1 John 1:6–7, 2:6), and growing to be like him (1 John 4:17), there is no reason to be guilt-laden or confidence-lacking. Let us resolve to stand up to the questions of others with a godly humility/confidence just like Jesus. Right now there are questions, questions, questions. One day there will only be answers, answers, answers. Bring on that day!

Questions for Reflection

1. What undermines your confidence? Is it a past sin, a difficulty in accepting forgiveness, fear of what others think, or something else? Will you surrender whatever it is to God?
2. What is the most powerful part of your personal experience with God? How can you share it with people who don't know God so that it comes across as relevant to them?
3. Why is being questioned a good thing? How does it help you?

Prayer

Father of answers, help me not to be afraid of questions. After all, I have a few questions of my own. Strengthen me to accept the ones that will not be answered in this life. Help me to be glad when people ask me questions, and help me answer them with salty grace. Teach me how to answer as Jesus would. In his name I ask this, Amen.

9

An Ophthalmologic Opportunity

John Chapter 9

What is the worst thing about being blind? Walking into lamp-posts? Putting on socks that don't match? Being vulnerable to mug-gers and con artists? Never seeing the faces of your wife or children whom you love so much? In the days of Jesus blindness was so much worse an affliction than it is today. No braille, no guide dogs, no cataract surgery, no possibility ever of cure! You were defenseless, worthless and usually penniless. I don't know what I would miss the most if I went blind. But I am sure of one thing—I would want to know *why* it had happened! I would be asking the doctors, the nurs-es and especially I would be asking God.

My heart sank as I heard the recent radio report of another earth-quake near the island of Sumatra. Many have died, although at least this time the area was spared the horrors of a tsunami. We wonder why such things happen. This is not a new question. The early dis-ciples also wanted to know the theological background to suffering. They asked Jesus, "Rabbi, who sinned, this man or his parents, that he was born blind?" (v2).

Cause and Effect?

In both Old and New Testament times, the assumption was that suffering was the result of sin. This is illustrated in the book of Job where Eliphaz said, "Consider now: Who, being innocent, has ever perished? Where were the upright ever destroyed? As I have observed, those who plow evil and those who sow trouble reap it" (Job 4:7–8). The implication of Eliphaz was that Job's suffering was the result of some hidden sin.

Likewise, the Pharisees said to the man born blind, "You were steeped in sin at birth; how dare you lecture us!" (v34). They saw a direct link between his blindness and sin. We may balk at this now, but before we become too self-righteous, it may be well to reflect on how we react to hearing of the suffering of others. Is it with unreserved compassion, or with a desire to gossip over the possible hidden root cause of their affliction?

The View of Jesus

Jesus is careful not to imply that all suffering is due to sin. In Luke's Gospel he says,

> Now there were some present at that time who told Jesus about the Galileans whose blood Pilate had mixed with their sacrifices. Jesus answered, "Do you think that these Galileans were worse sinners than all the other Galileans because they suffered this way? I tell you, no! But unless you repent, you too will all perish. Or those eighteen who died when the tower in Siloam fell on them—do you think they were more guilty than all the others living in Jerusalem? I tell you, no! But unless you repent, you too will all perish." (Luke 13:1–5)

In John 9 he says, "Neither this man nor his parents sinned" (v3). Jesus then goes on to give the reason for this man's blindness: "But this happened so that the work of God might be displayed in his life" (v3). Clearly Jesus is saying there is a higher purpose to the blind man's suffering. God does not cause our suffering, but makes good use of it. We must be humble in assessing the reasons for suffering—whether it is our own or that of other people.

The Weird Love of Jesus

Can you imagine how the blind man felt when Jesus came up to him? There is no record of the man asking to be healed. Imagine a stranger grabbing you. Not only that, but what if he spat on the ground, made mud and smeared it all over your eyes?! Even given the fact that in those days the spit of a renowned person was thought to have special powers, it must have been really weird.

Jesus regularly broke through comfort zones and traditions to show the love and power of God. People often misunderstood this. The Pharisees said, "This man is not from God, for he does not keep the Sabbath" (v16). Actually, Jesus wasn't breaking the law, but he was breaking a *tradition* about the Sabbath law. The Pharisees got really worked up about such things because they loved the law. This is no bad thing. The Psalmist says, "Oh, how I love your law! I meditate on it all day long" (Psalm 119:97). The problem is when we use man-made bolt-ons to the law to judge people. A lecturer I know illustrated it this way:

> Two Pharisees are driving down the motorway. The speed limit is 70 mph. A true Pharisee would never break this limit, so Jacob says to Aaron, "Let's drive at 65 mph just in case the speedometer isn't working properly."
>
> "OK," says Aaron, "but what if there is a sudden gust of wind behind us? We'd better drive at 60 just in case."
>
> "Good point," says Jacob, "but also, what if I sneeze and my foot stabs on the accelerator? We'd better stick to 55 mph."
>
> "Problem solved," says Aaron. "Now we're sure to keep within the law."
>
> Having dropped their speed to the law-safe 55 mph a car passes them in the outside lane doing 65 mph.
>
> "Filthy, Samaritan-loving, Molech-worshipping, pork-eating Gentile law-breakers!" they cry in unison.

Jesus was not breaking the law. He was revealing God's compassion and power. The problem is the next question.

Who Is Really Blind Here?

Surely John had a twinkle in his eye as he wrote chapter 9! The humor in the passage is so strong. I would love to have been a fly on the wall listening to the dialogue between the (formerly) blind man and the Pharisees as they got tied in theological knots (9:24–34). John wants us to "see" the "blindness" of the Pharisees. Why is this? Is it because John has a thing against Pharisees? Perhaps one trod on his foot when he was a little boy? No, I don't think so. Perhaps it is because John knows that *we* can be just as blind. *No, not me! I was blind but now I see!* Sure, but are you *certain* there is not even a *bit* of blindness in you?

My own blindness is revealed when I am judgmental, when I make assumptions. The first time I came to the church I said to myself, "This can't be a real church. There is no organ, no stained-glass windows or dog collars and (most importantly) they don't sing the hymns I know." I soon came to realize that these are not the substance of "church," but it is hard to avoid judging things based on assumption-tinted first impressions. If you are new to church, could I make an appeal that you suspend your judgments about the externals until you've had a good chance to examine the internals of what it means to be a follower of Jesus and a member of his body, the church?

What about those of us who have been in Christ for a while? For example, have you ever had any of these thoughts? "He/she can't be doing well spiritually because he/she drives a Mercedes/holidays abroad/wears make-up/wasn't here last week/has dirty shoes…" We have an obligation to one another and the Lord to hate our self-righteousness. This does not mean we stand far off from one another and do nothing about what we see. "See no evil, hear no evil, speak no evil" is not appropriate. (Well, "speak no evil" is, but not the others!) If we see brothers or sisters in sin, we'd better heed Hebrews 3:12–13 and Galatians 6:1. The caution is simply that we do not pass judgment until we know the facts—*all* the facts. Just as it would be wrong to assume that someone who missed a Sunday service was in deep sin, had sold their soul to the devil, and had participated in child-sacrifice, it would be equally wrong to assume that someone who attended once a month was doing just fine and dandy.

How is your assumption radar? Are you picking up your own ill-informed judgments? Have you got a handle on where you might make judgments based merely on appearances (John 7:24)? Ask God to open your eyes, and prepare for a surprise!

The Right Worship

It would be wrong however, to focus only on this one aspect of the passage. Here we are seeing an awesome demonstration of God's power through Jesus. And the response of the man born blind? "He worshiped him" (v38). Did you notice the progression of this man's faith? He starts by knowing him as an anonymous Rabbi, then comes to experience him as a healer, finds out from others he is called Jesus (v11), comes to the conviction he is a prophet (v17), develops the belief he came from God (v33), discovers he is the Son of Man (vv35–37), acknowledges him as Lord and therefore *worships* him (v38)!

Am I stating the obvious when I say it is easy to lose sight of who we are following? We get busy, distracted and tired. After a gradual process of drifting (Hebrews 2:1), we wake up one day and realize we are in a bad place. Prayer is a pain, Bible study a burden, and church a chore. How did this happen? It happened when other things got in the way of us seeing Jesus. We *become* blind (to all intents and purposes) because we are not determinedly focused on our Lord. I have a motto: "When in doubt, worship!"

Sometimes I do not know what to do or say. I am confused about the best decision to make. What to do? I go to my piano and sing hymns and choruses to my Lord. I sing and play until I feel different. "Feel different?!" I hear you cry. "You mean it's all about how you feel?" No. I mean I sing, play and worship until I am reconnected to my Lord, the great Shepherd and Overseer of my soul (1 Peter 2:25). You don't have to be a pianist (I'm only very average as it is), but if you lift your voice and heart to the God of glory you'll become conscious of his presence and power in your life.

The only correct response to the power and love of Jesus is to worship him as Lord. The man born blind shows us this. John records it for us so that we remember it.

To go back to the start of this chapter—what are the worst things about being blind? Perhaps two things. First, thinking you can see without realizing you are blind. In this case, no one can help you. Second, being healed of blindness and becoming blind once again. What a tragedy! The glory of John chapter 9 is that we find the answers to recovery of sight for the spiritually blind (Luke 4:18) initially and throughout our lives.

Questions for Reflection

1. What is the greatest test in your life right now? Are you blaming God for anything? Do you find it difficult to trust that "the work of God" (v3) will be displayed in this situation? Can you pray for such faith?
2. Are you aware of your assumptions, prejudices and fears? Can you ask God and friends to help you see them?
3. Is worship a priority? Will you put some time aside *today* to worship, to reconnect and enjoy being with your Lord?

Prayer

Father, thank you that Jesus has given me sight. I am so grateful the great eye-surgeon has operated on the eyes of my soul. Help me see more and more clearly, never developing the cataracts of super-spirituality or self-righteousness. Strengthen my life of worship. Make me fully aware of your presence and power. In the name of Jesus the Sight-Bringer, Amen.

10

A Nation of Sheep-Keepers

John Chapter 10

Have you spent much time around sheep? Although I grew up in the countryside, I had little to do with sheep. Where I lived they farmed apples and oats, and raised cows. The nearest most of us come to sheep these days is in Tesco's frozen-food aisle. A leg of lamb makes for a tasty Sunday lunch!

What do you think of sheep? Pretty dumb animals, right? I am not too encouraged by the imagery here that clearly likens me, a follower of Jesus, to a sheep! Can't I be an eagle, a great white shark, or a lion (king of the beasts!)? Actually, sheep aren't as thick as we think. Research in Cambridge has shown they can remember the faces of fifty other sheep for up to two years.[1] They are also capable of problem-solving. Sheep in Yorkshire foiled a cattle grid that was keeping them from some tasty plants, flowers and vegetables in villagers' gardens. They taught themselves to roll eight feet across the hoof-proof metal grids by lying down on their sides and rolling over and over until they reached the other side! Clever, don't you think?! They've even learned how to hurdle five-foot high fences and squeeze through gaps as small as eight inches.[2]

Anyway, I suppose if Jesus says I am a sheep, I should be happy about it. Maybe that is the point. It is not so much that *I* am a sheep as the fact that *he* is my Shepherd.

The people of Jesus' day had a great affinity with sheep. Many

---

1. "The 'Intelligent' Side of Sheep": BBC online article (Wednesday, 7 November, 2001).
2. "Crafty Sheep Conquer Cattle Grids": BBC online article (Friday, 30 July, 2004).

were sheep farmers or came from families where sheep farming was common. The imagery used by Jesus was scattered throughout the Old Testament; it was something that both the crowds and the Pharisees would have understood. The children of Jacob were sheep farmers (Genesis 47:3), and so it could almost be said that the people of Israel were a nation of sheep-keepers (which recalls Napoleon's remark that "England is a nation of shopkeepers"). Sheep and everything sheepy was part of their language and culture.

How do we get into the mind of Jesus and his hearers? One way is to have a look at some of the Old Testament teaching about shepherds.

Good Shepherd/Bad Shepherd

The Old Testament prophets used loads of sheep and shepherd imagery to teach God's people about their relationship with him and his expectations of their leaders. Zechariah is typical of this and probably forms the background to Jesus' thinking as he teaches in John 10. For example, Zechariah 11:17 says,

> "Woe to the worthless shepherd,
>   who deserts the flock!
> May the sword strike his arm and his right eye!
>   May his arm be completely withered, his right eye
>   totally blinded!"

Jesus is contrasting his style of "shepherding" with that of the Pharisees, who have so consistently opposed his teaching and claims. He is the shepherd who lays down his life for the sheep, as prophesied in Zechariah 12:10:

> "They will look on me, the one they have pierced, and they
> will mourn for him as one mourns for an only child, and
> grieve bitterly for him as one grieves for a firstborn son."

The classic chapter about spiritual shepherding is in Ezekiel 34. Here are a few selected quotes that contrast the wicked shepherds of

Israel with God himself as the chief shepherd:

> "Woe to the shepherds of Israel who only take care of them-
> selves! ...You eat the curds, clothe yourselves with the wool
> and slaughter the choice animals, but you do not take care of
> the flock. You have not strengthened the weak or healed the
> sick or bound up the injured. You have not brought back the
> strays or searched for the lost. You have ruled them harshly
> and brutally.... My sheep wandered over all the mountains....
> They were scattered..., and no one searched or looked for
> them.... (vv2–4, 6)
> "For this is what the Sovereign LORD says: I myself will
> search for my sheep and look after them. ...I will rescue
> them.... I will...tend them in a good pasture...they will lie
> down in good grazing land.... I will search for the lost and
> bring back the strays. I will bind up the injured and strength-
> en the weak.... I will shepherd the flock with justice....
> (vv11,12b, 14, 16)
> I will save my flock.... I will place over them one shepherd,
> my servant David.... He will tend them and be their shepherd.
> I the LORD will be their God, and my servant David will be
> prince among them. I the LORD have spoken." (vv22–23)

With this understanding of how God views spiritual shepherding, let's now go back and have a look at what Jesus is saying in John
chapter 10 and what John is hoping we will grasp.

The Good Shepherd's Heart
John shows us that the heart of Jesus is the heart of God—one
of self-sacrificial love for his sheep. The key verse in the chapter is,
"The good shepherd lays down his life for the sheep" (v11). This is
a prediction of what Jesus did indeed go on to do (Revelation
5:6–14). Since Jesus' sacrifice is the reality under which we live,
what should our response be?

Follow the Flautist
Not only do sheep remember the face of other sheep, but they
remember their shepherd. One Bible commentator recounts this story,

...Arab shepherds are well known for knowing their sheep personally. During the Palestinian uprising in the late 1980s the Israeli army decided to punish a village near Bethlehem for not paying its taxes (which, the village claimed, simply financed their occupation). The officer in command rounded up all of the village animals and placed them in a large barbed-wire pen.

Later in the week he was approached by a woman who begged him to release her flock, arguing that since her husband was dead, the animals were her only source of livelihood. He pointed to the pen containing hundreds of animals and humorously quipped that it was impossible because he could not find her animals. She asked that if she could in fact separate them herself, would he be willing to let her take them? He agreed. A soldier opened the gate and the woman's son produced a small reed flute. He played a simple tune again and again—and soon sheep heads began popping up across the pen. The young boy continued his music and walked home, followed by his flock of twenty-five sheep.[3]

Now that's the kind of pied piper I don't mind following! There are a couple of questions that come to my mind when I think about these facts. Firstly, if Jesus knows us by name, have I forgotten how lucky I am to be in his flock? Am I trying to run away, or am I grateful for the way he "hems me in" (Psalm 139:5) for my protection and safety?[4] The devil is like a "roaring lion looking for someone to devour" (1 Peter 5:8). The lion is real. I have a place of safety in a world of savagery. Remember Psalm 23?

> The LORD is my shepherd, I shall not be in want.
>   He makes me lie down in green pastures,
> he leads me beside quiet waters,
>   he restores my soul.
> He guides me in paths of righteousness
>   for his name's sake.
> Even though I walk
>   through the valley of the shadow of death,
> I will fear no evil,

---

3. Gary M. Burge, *NIV Application Commentary, Book of John* (Grand Rapids: Zondervan, 2000, electronic edition), 302.

4. Check out *The Message* version of that verse: "I look behind me and you're there, then up ahead and you're there, too—your reassuring presence, coming and going."

for you are with me;
your rod and your staff,
    they comfort me.

You prepare a table before me
    in the presence of my enemies.
You anoint my head with oil;
    my cup overflows.
Surely goodness and love will follow me
    all the days of my life,
and I will dwell in the house of the LORD
        forever.

Why kick against such love? Something that always helps is to consider where we would be without Christ. This was brought home to me recently when my wife and I had a conversation at the dinner table with our two teenage children. One of the children asked my wife, "Mum, what would our lives be like if you and Dad hadn't become Christians?"

My wife replied, "You wouldn't exist!" She went on to explain how our deep-rooted selfishness would have caused us to divorce long before having kids. She was right, of course. I know my sins would have driven my wife mad (well, even madder!) and taken us to the divorce court. What a stark reminder of the impact of Jesus on our lives! Not only would my wife and I be living with the pain of a broken marriage, but also two people we love so dearly *wouldn't even exist!*

Here is a suggestion—take some time today to imagine where you might be in your life, marriage, parenting, career, relationships and health without the guidance of Jesus? Write it down and offer a prayer of gratitude.

Second, if Jesus is calling us, do we hear his voice? One of the challenges of the Christian life is to remain attentive to Jesus as he speaks to us. I am not talking about only one source of his voice either. The main way Jesus guides us is through the Word (Psalm 119:105), but he is constantly teaching us through the circumstances of life. This was how Paul understood challenging situations in his life (2 Corinthians 1:9), his dreams (Acts 16:9) and unanswered prayers (2 Corinthians 12:7–10). What is God doing in your life right now? How is he communicating his will to you? Take some time to reflect on what is happening in your personal, spiritual and professional life. Pray to hear the flute and follow its lead.

Leading or Driving?

We are safe and secure in his care. Why would we ever want to leave the one who lays down his life for us? The shepherd is leading his flock, not driving it. A story I heard some time ago illustrates this point.

It seems that a group of western tourists were on a coach-tour of the Holy Land. Passing through the Judean countryside, their tour guide was keen to give them some local cultural flavor. He did this by contrasting the norms of western and Middle Eastern customs. "For example," the guide said, "in the west sheep are *driven* by the shepherd, whereas here the shepherd *leads* his sheep." This was intended to indicate the more intimate relationship between sheep and shepherd in this part of the world.

However, after the guide had said this, a sharp-eyed tourist called the guide's attention to something they had seen through the window of the coach. "Look," he said, "there is a shepherd now. And he is *driving* the flock of sheep. What you have just told us is untrue!"

The tour guide immediately ordered the coach to stop, jumped off and ran over to talk to the man driving the sheep. A short conversation ensued and the guide came back to the coach with a big smile on his face. Clambering back onto the coach, he took the microphone and announced to the curious tourists, "That man driving the sheep isn't the shepherd. He's the butcher!"

We are led by a shepherd, not driven by a butcher! How are you feeling about being led by Jesus Christ? I think we follow willingly when we are inspired, but we struggle to make progress when we are driven. Much of this has to do with the way we are led by our human leaders in church. But to be mature, we have to grow beyond our circumstances to find our deeper motivation in Christ. Whether my earthly leaders are leading in a good or bad way, I can still find my inspiration in Jesus. If he is my Shepherd I have nothing to fear.

The Choice

In this chapter we see that Jesus sets out his stall, making it clear what he is offering and what he is expecting. He is the good Shepherd. If we are in his flock, we will be well fed and watered, protected and guided. But it is our choice. Many around Jesus did not accept his call. They refused to trust him and so missed out on these blessings. Have you made your choice? If you decided to follow Jesus the Shepherd some time ago, are you still devoted to him? Let me plead with you not to give up on him. If you have never made this decision, let me encourage you to let him be the gate to a full life (v10).

Perhaps we can imitate Jesus' Shepherd heart for someone we know. Can you sacrifice some of your time, energy or money for them? This is what changes people and our world. Love defined by sacrifice.

Questions for Reflection

1. Are you listening to the flautist? What direction is Jesus calling you in?
2. Are you feeling led or driven by Jesus? Why?
3. Do you have a decision to make regarding following Jesus?

Prayer

Father, thank you that Jesus shows me the way into your sheepfold. Thank you I can trust the tune Jesus plays. Help me to hear his voice and follow his lead. Help me bring others to the gate of eternal life. In the name of Jesus, the great Shepherd of my soul, Amen.

11

Die to Live Another Day

John Chapter 11

Have you ever seen a dead body? I am sorry if I'm reawakening bad memories, but death is a taboo subject today in many cultures. Often the quickest way to silence your work colleagues is to bring up one of two topics—"Jesus" or "death." It wasn't always this way. Historically most cultures have encountered death as a natural and normal part of life. Until very recently in the developed parts of the world, parents simply accepted that a number of their children would die. Advances in medicine mean we expect an improved survival rate. That is a good thing, but there is an unfortunate side effect: We tend to think less often about the deeper things in life.

At a funeral recently a friend who had been drifting in her faith came to me and said, "I've got to get to grips with my spiritual life again." When the mother of a disciple died last year, the disciple came to me and said, "I'd like you to help me get my spiritual life back on track. I need to use this event to revitalize my faith." One changed and the other didn't, but death prompted both to do a life-check. This kind of soberness is needed in our lives from time to time. I think it is no coincidence that John records this event in detail. He does so for more than one reason, which we will look at below. But before we get into the story itself, here are two bits of background that I hope will deepen our appreciation of this amazing chapter.

The Seven Signs

The raising of Lazarus from the dead is the seventh and final sign that John records Jesus performing. See the following list of the signs in John's Gospel:

1. Changing water into wine (2:1–11)
2. Cleansing the temple (2:13–22)
3. Healing the royal official's son (4:46–54)
4. Healing the lame man (5:1–15)
5. Feeding the five thousand (5:1–15)
6. Healing the blind man (9:1–41)
7. Raising Lazarus to life (11:1–44)

These seven signs (seven being the number of perfection in Jewish thinking) show Jesus as the one authorized by God to lead his people into the light and set them free. He was setting them truly free—not from Roman domination, but from spiritual blindness and bondage (see also Luke 4:18–21).

The Foreshadowing

The raising of Lazarus clearly foreshadows Jesus' own resurrection. This is proven partly from what he does in raising Lazarus to life (vv43–44), partly in what he says ("I am the resurrection and the life"—v25) and partly in what his opponents prophesy ("It is better for you that one man die for the people than that the whole nation perish"—v50). The historical fact of Jesus' resurrection is central to the message of the gospel (1 Corinthians 15:1–20) and something we should never forget.

I don't know about you, but I am better at defending some aspects of Christian teachings than others. One area we all ought to be good at defending and explaining is the resurrection. Could you give a good account of this event to a skeptic? As a young Christian this might be a challenge, but it shouldn't take us long to learn how to do this effectively. There are many helpful books and Web sites around.[1]

---

1. Josh McDowell, *The Resurrection Factor* (Nashville: Thomas Nelson, 1993); Frank Morrison, *Who Moved the Stone–Reprint Edition* (Grand Rapids: Zondervan, 1987); J. Wenham, *Easter Enigma* (Eugene, OR: Wipf & Stock Publishers, 2005); and www.douglasjacoby.com, to suggest a few.

However, nothing helps you want to learn more than that glorious feeling of being "stumped" in a discussion. One of the best things that can ever happen to you is to be explaining the resurrection to someone when the person you are teaching asks a question you can't answer. What do we do then? "Oh, No! I've brought the whole gospel into disrepute because I don't know the answer!" Keep your hair on. No one knows *all* the answers (except God). Not knowing an answer is a tremendous opportunity to say, "Great question. I don't know the answer, but I promise that by the next time you see me I'll have had a good look into it and be ready to give you my best shot." The thing that impresses most people is not omnipotence (which is a pretense), but humility.

With those thoughts in the background, let's now move on to discuss what this passage teaches us about God, Jesus and ourselves.

Jesus' Timing Makes Sure God Gets the Glory

How often have we prayed something like this: "Oh God, please give me patience. And give it to me NOW!"

The Bible is littered with examples of people who didn't get what they wanted when they wanted it. Abraham and Sarah waited longer than they hoped before Isaac was born. The proverbial phrase, "the patience of Job" is still in our language for a reason! The man born blind from our previous chapter must have wondered, after his healing, why God waited until he was an adult before sending Jesus to cure him.

In all these situations and more, the point is that God got the glory (9:3). God sets the times and places so that we will find him and so that he will be revealed as the one with the power (Acts 17:26–27). In this way more and more people will see God's glory and, he hopes, be drawn to him.

So why did Jesus wait two more days and arrive on the fourth day of death? Most likely because it was commonly thought that a dead person's spirit would revisit the body during the three days following death to see if there was any possibility of resuscitation. After three days the spirit left, never to return. Jesus waits until the fourth day to *really* amaze the people. There could be no doubt in anyone's mind that this was an incredible miracle—Lazarus was not just dead, he was *really* dead!

Is there something in your life that you think God should have dealt with already or should have kept from happening? Something you are frustrated about? Are you tempted to take matters into your own hands, to go for the Genesis 16 Hagar solution? Does it feel to you, as I think it seemed to Mary and Martha, that Jesus doesn't care (vv21, 32)?

- God gets the glory when we patiently wait for a Christian spouse.
- God gets the glory when we are honest, even when it makes us look bad.
- God gets the glory when we forgive despite being unappreciated.
- God gets the glory when we don't retaliate despite having justice on our side.
- God gets the glory when we return insults with blessings.
- God gets the glory when we are persecuted yet rejoice.
- God gets the glory when others are promoted over our heads and we congratulate them.
- God gets the glory when our younger sister is married before us and we are thrilled.
- God gets the glory when someone gets the credit due to us and we don't offer a correction of the facts.
- God gets the glory when we give to the poor when we can't afford it.

How can God be glorified in your life right now? Take a moment to fill in the following:

God can be glorified in my life by

_____

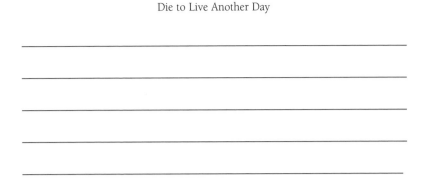

It is important for us to bear in mind that God's "delay" is not indifference, but patience (2 Peter 3:9). He knows the best time for everything, so let's pray to *enjoy* his patience and not just *endure* it!

The Heart of the Resurrector

Have you noticed something curious about chapter 11? It seems to be about Lazarus—but he doesn't speak a single word! What does this tell us? It reveals that it is really *all about Jesus!* So what are we meant to see here about Jesus? What do John and the Holy Spirit want us to observe? Perhaps there are two things: Jesus' power and Jesus' compassion. First, let's talk about his compassion.

Jesus is "deeply moved in spirit and troubled" (v33), he weeps (v35) and is again "deeply moved" (v38). As someone put it, "What a beautiful display of Jesus' full humanity at the threshold of the most amazing display of his divinity."[2] Our Christianity must never be reduced to simply a set of doctrines. We are loved by a fiercely compassionate God. We are saved by the self-sacrificial love of Jesus Christ.

You and I may not be able to physically raise the dead, but we can take the pain of our friends to heart. Our call is not to be a resurrector but a conveyor of compassion—personally showing people the practical Christlike compassion they so desperately need. As his disciples we enjoy and glory in his love, and therefore we should imitate it. After the parable of the Good Samaritan Jesus said, "Go and do likewise" (Luke 10:37). What aspect of "likewise" are you practicing?

There are many different types of pain being felt by our neighbors

2. Andreas Kostenberger, *Encountering John: The Gospel in Historical, Literary, and Theological Perspective* (Nashville: Baker Academic, 2002), 131.

—physical, emotional and spiritual. Perhaps you can visit people in prison like some friends of mine do. On the other hand you could join a bereavement support group and enter into the pain of others by "being there" with them. My experience of being trained by a bereavement visiting service was life changing. How about spending time with someone in the hospital? I will leave it to you to fill in the blanks, but let's not leave a blank.

I could show Christlike compassion to

_____

by

_____

_____

_____

The Power of the Resurrector

Jesus not only *gives* life, he *is* life! We have this life in the future *and* now! (See John 5:21, 25–29; 6:40.) How do we get this life? We get it at baptism (Romans 6:3–5), and we will keep it when we die (Romans 6:9, 1 Corinthians 15:21ff). Do you think much about this? Paul encourages the Thessalonians to talk about the life to come, and he signs off his teaching on the subject with the phrase, "Therefore encourage each other with these words" (1 Thessalonians 4:18).

I will never forget the first time I really thought and talked about what heaven might be like. It was the summer of 1986. About ten of us had been very busy over the summer using all our spare time to invite people to a series of evangelistic meetings. The weather was hot, and our feet were sore. The leader of our group was George. One day, sensing we were tired, he suggested we retire to a café. Now this café in Queens' Park, London, was not the most salubrious culinary establishment known to man. It was greasy, smoky and dark. If you liked grease with your grease (which I did at the time), you were going to enjoy yourself.

We sat at the back of the café and ordered lunch. George introduced the topic of heaven to the conversation and it was as if we had been transported to another place of sweetness, cleanliness and delight. In a trice the dankness of our surroundings faded as person after person shared their vision of heaven. Bible verses were read, imagination ran wild, speculation was rife, and we were in another world! One talked of what it might be like to meet God face to face for the first time; another spoke of the fellowship. I shared about my vision of the huge heavenly choirs and gargantuan orchestras playing music like we'd never heard and yet that seemed strangely familiar (I'm a musician by training). I could hear the music as I described the scene to the people around me, and, even as I write this (though it was twenty years ago), the hairs of my neck are standing on end as I recall the discussion, the excitement, the feeling and the vision of heaven we generated between us!

I left that café a different man. The time flew by; the rest of the day passed as if in a dream, and I soon invited someone to one of the meetings who became a Christian and is responsible for a lengthy family tree of disciples that is still growing to this day. When I get tired of the Christian life (yes, it is possible), I try to remember the life hereafter and put things in perspective. I *will* die—and that's a good thing!

Look, think about it from Lazarus' perspective. I mean, after Jesus brought him back to life, how do you think he felt about death? I imagine that years later Lazarus contracts some fatal disease or other. Mary and Martha gather beside his deathbed. Instead of worried sisters' furrowed brows, smiles come to their lips as all three realize they've been here before. Mary says, "Do you remember what a hard time I gave Jesus?"

Martha says, "Yeah. He really confused me with that 'I am the resurrection' stuff." And Lazarus, ah, Lazarus, he says, "Where's a Messiah when you need one. You just can't get good help these days!" They all have a good laugh.

The moment comes for Lazarus to close his eyes for the last

time—not in panic and fear as in the first death, but with a relaxed peace. Mary and Martha are sad, desperately sad to see their brother die, but there is no wailing, no recrimination, no fear. They had been here before, but now there is a difference. Jesus is not distant, but he is *with* Lazarus in death! And in knowing this, Lazarus also knows Jesus will be with him in his resurrection. What is Lazarus thinking as he closes his eyes? I don't know, but one thing I'm pretty sure of is that his "second life" (the life between his first death and his second) was a life characterized by peace, joy and certitude as to his destiny. I like to think he lived the kind of freedom that most people can only dream of. He knew where he was going, and he knew who was taking him there.

Why do we fret about our lives? Why do we fight so hard for life? Perhaps because we are not thinking straight about the purpose of life and the fact we serve the one who conquered death and made sense of the grave. Because I know I will die, I am liberated in this life to live with freedom and joy. Do you want to live without fear? Then think about death more often—and about what comes next!

Questions for Reflection

1. When was the last time you felt deeply moved for someone in trouble? Is there someone you know in pain? Will you pray to have compassion for them?
2. What could you do this week for someone in pain? Send a card, make a phone call, visit? Something else?
3. Is there anything in life you fear? Why? Try reading Romans chapter 8 and praying through it.

Prayer

Father, you are my Creator. You gave me life. Thank you for every second you've granted me on this earth. Help me to remember this world is not my home so I won't get too attached to it. Give me a vision of the next life that will keep me excited about this one. I pray to face death with peace and live life to the full. In Jesus' name, Amen.

12

Scent of Glory

John Chapter 12

My physical education teacher, Mr. "Wally" Watson, had a very effective way of recruiting volunteers. He would line us all up against the changing room wall and say, "I need three volunteers." Then he'd point at us and say, "You, you and you." The three hapless victims would then troop out onto the playing fields to whatever onerous task lay before them.

Jesus, however, was not an unwilling victim; he volunteered for the job. The importance of his impending death is emphasized by the fact that Mary's amazing sacrifice is given only one verse (v3), while the discussion of Judas' motives and Jesus' explanation that this was a preparation for his burial are given five verses (vv4–8). If I were Mary reading this later, I'd be tempted to have a word with John. "Hang on," I'd say. "That perfume cost me a year's wages. That's a lot of dosh! I even wiped Jesus' feet with my hair—and you jolly well know it is a disgraceful thing for a woman to let down her hair in public. Not only that, but I washed his feet—which ought to be done by a servant. You should have given me more screen time!"

It does seem a bit strange that we don't have more detail about this event. But when we see that John, with a film director's perspective, is making sure that Jesus remains center screen, we begin to understand why he doesn't elaborate more on Mary's act of devotion.

Here's a little question: When you do something "big" for God or for people, are you okay with not getting much credit? On second thought, maybe it is a *big* question! Jesus taught, "Then your Father, who sees what is done in secret, will reward you" (Matthew 6:6). My friend Archie used to say to me, "I want to be *more* in private than I am in public." He lived it out, too—something I find challenging, to say the least!

Somehow I don't think Mary was thinking of her historic legacy when she went to the market, poured out a pile of shekels so high that it made the stall-holder's eyes pop out on cartoon stalks, splashed the perfume over Jesus and did the first-century equivalent of the Timotei shampoo girl's hair-washing motion down on the floor.

One commentator put it this way,

> This story is all about devotion, and Mary is the perfect charac-
> ter to model this. Wherever she appears both in this Gospel
> and in Luke, she appears at Jesus' feet. This is a symbol of her
> interest as a devoted disciple of Jesus, and it is significant that
> Jesus defends her, giving her a respected place as one who
> knows better even than Jesus' apostles.... It is likely that Jesus
> kept this scent on his body through the following week. When
> he was suffering the anguish of crucifixion, Mary's gift
> remained. It was the last truly beautiful fragrance he smelled as
> he went to the cross.[1]

Saintly Smells

Our acts of service are similar expressions of devotion to Jesus. It is clear in Romans 12, for example, that serving the Lord and serv-ing one another are not separate activities, but each is an expression of the other. The Philippians' gift to Paul is described as a "fragrant offering" (Philippians 4:18), and our prayers are "golden bowls full of incense" (Revelation 5:8). Do you like to smell good? My wife smells good to me—and I try to smell good to her! More important-ly, I'd like to smell good to my Lord. How does this happen? What is the cosmic "Eau de Cologne"?

My spiritual "Chanel No. 7" (it has to be seven since this is the number of perfection in the Bible) is serving God through serving

---

1. Gary M. Burge, *NIV Application Commentary, Book of John* (Grand Rapids: Zondervan, 2000), 335–361.

others without doing so under human compulsion (2 Corinthians 9:7), but compelled by the love of Christ (2 Corinthians 5:14). In doing this we offer a sweet aroma that God breathes in deeply. It brings a smile to his face. Every time a disciple denies him or herself for the sake of another human being and the gospel, the Father turns to Jesus and the Spirit and says, "Can you smell that? That is the fragrant perfume of the deeds of the saints. I *love* that smell!"

Did Mary feel compelled? Yes and no. No, because no one forced her against her will. Yes, because she was compelled by the love she had for her Lord, her friend, the resurrector of her brother. She knew Jesus loved her and though probably unknowingly, she was thanking him for the ultimate sacrifice he was about to offer for her and for the whole world.

Squirming Sacrifices

We get far too hung up on this compulsion issue (well, *I* do). "Do I *have* to share my faith? Do I *have* to pray? Do I *have* to come to church? What do I have to do to be saved, stay saved, make sure of my place in heaven, stay in God's good book, etc.?" Have you ever thought like this? It is natural enough, but it is so sad. We are meant to be willing servants. I remember a sermon on this topic I heard over twenty years ago. It was on the passage in Romans 12:1, which commands us to "offer your bodies as living sacrifices." I remember the preacher saying, "The problem with living sacrifices is that they tend to squirm off the altar." We are living sacrifices, willing slaves, so how do we keep our willingness fresh?

When my kids were small and had started to walk, they unwittingly demonstrated to me the meaning of compulsion by love instead of duty. It was a common occurrence that I would be sitting somewhere in the house and they would disturb me. I might be reading, talking on the phone, or even counseling someone when they would totter into my presence looking for Daddy. No matter the atmosphere in the room they would come to my side and stretch their arms out wide. This wordless gesture spoke louder and more clearly than any argument. They were saying, "Pick me up, Daddy. I want a hug!" How could I ever refuse? I could never shoo them away. Such spontaneous expressions of love *compelled* me to reach down, pick them up, and cradle them in my arms. I couldn't help myself. I treasured those moments and still treasure the memories.

When we ask the "What do I *have* to do...?" question, we are missing the point. We are forgetting what has been done for us and why. Jesus died for us because he *wanted* to. He was a willing volunteer, and so I am a willing follower and imitator.

We may never know the full impact of our voluntary service. I am sure Mary had no idea we would be talking about what she did 2,000 years later. God takes what we do and multiplies its effectiveness. What might God be able to do with your service? Only he knows, but, by faith, we can act and then trust he will make more of it than we expect. Why not do something *today*?

Donkey-Taxi

Why did Jesus ride into the city on a donkey? Surely the King of Glory deserves air conditioning, power steering, air bags, ABS and, at the very least, smoked glass. Okay, so they weren't available, but where is the noble steed with bejeweled harness and gold stirrups? There could be several reasons why Jesus traveled by donkey-taxi. One that occurs to me is that the horse was seen as a beast of war, while a donkey symbolized peace. Jesus wanted to make it clear that while he was a victorious king, he was also a humble champion of peace. A good lesson for us! We like to win and to be seen to win.

I spoke harshly to my daughter recently, rebuking her over watching too much television. My wife brought to my attention that I may have been a little overbearing. I was having none of it and justified my behavior with many fine-sounding arguments. They didn't convince me, let alone her, but they kept her at bay while I licked my wounds. Later I apologized to them both. Why was I so stubborn? Why did I want to "win" the argument? Because I was too insecure to listen with an open heart and mind. How unlike Jesus.

Jesus was confident of his final victory over death and sin, and his security came from knowing he was totally surrendered to God's will (vv23–28). Therefore, how he looked to those around him did not matter. Do you wish to have a deeper assurance of God's love for you and not to care what others think? I guess we all do! You can. It is a matter of getting to know God better and better through your years as a Christian. There are many things that help with this, but let me for now mention just one.

Time

Depth takes openness, trust, vulnerability and many other things, but the one thing that must be added to all of this is time. One incentive to persevere in the Christian life is simply that as time goes by, we are more able to look back and see how God used the circumstances of our lives to develop depth in our Christian character and our relationship with him. As time goes by, we will gain a deeper surety of our salvation and confidence in the grace that is ours in Christ (Hebrews 4:15–16).

Are you facing a challenge to your trust in God? Are you doubting his final victory? Take a good look at the way Jesus trusted his Father. He calmly rides a donkey to his God-ordained doom. Let us all pray to have that confidence—it *can* be yours.

Greeks and Glory

The term "Greeks" in verse 20 probably means God-fearing Gentiles. Perhaps they spoke to Philip because he had a Greek name, and they thought he would be more sympathetic to them. In any case, Jesus uses the opportunity to ram home his central message: Glory belongs to God and to me in the cross that is to come. The other Gospel writers tend to emphasize the cross as the place of suffering. It is noticeable that in John's Gospel (where there is no mention of the agonized prayers in Gethsemane) the emphasis is not so much on glory *through* the cross but glory *in* the cross. It is the *place* of Jesus' glorification. Why is this so important? Because "it is at the cross that Jesus is revealed as the fully obedient Son of the Father who faithfully accomplishes his mission."[2]

How can I bring glory to God? By persevering to the end? Yes,

---

2. Andreas Kostenberger, *Encountering John: The Gospel in Historical, Literary, and Theological Perspective* (Nashville: Baker Academic, 2002), 138.

but also by being faithful in the midst of the suffering between now and glory. It reminds me of the song, "Jesus, Keep Me Near the Cross." The words of the chorus say, "In the cross, in the cross, be my glory ever, till my longing soul shall find, peace beyond the river." If we can keep our eyes on the cross, we will not lose sight of the glory of God. Take the advice of John—gaze at, meditate on and rejoice in the glory of the cross and you will never lose your love for Jesus.

In Medias Res

And so we come to halftime. The end of chapter 12 closes the first half of the Gospel with neat symmetry. John started by proclaiming Jesus as "the light of all people. The light shines in the darkness, and the darkness did not overcome it" (1:4–5 NRSV). Towards the end of chapter 12 Jesus himself says, "I have come as light into the world, so that everyone who believes in me should not remain in the darkness" (v46 NRSV).

We have been taken on a roller-coaster tour of Jesus' miracles and teachings and seen how the people around him reacted. Some had faith, some skepticism, some hatred. We are prepared for the second half—the intimate teaching of the disciples and the crucifixion of the King of Glory. We are about to enter into the darkest yet most glorious phase of the earthly ministry of Jesus. Before we go on to this next and decisive phase, let me ask you to reflect on the lessons of chapter 12.

Questions for Reflection

1. When was the last time you did something extravagant for Jesus? Could you do something like this today?
2. Are you fully involved in serving others for the sake of the gospel? Could you volunteer for something? It may not bring you glory, but it will make God smile.
3. Is there something you are having a hard time trusting God with? What is the worst that could happen? Can God handle it? If he can—so can you!

Prayer

Father, thank you for the willing sacrifice of Jesus. Help me serve you and people around me with wholeheartedness. Teach me how to keep my motivation pure. Keep me confident and humble at the same time. Grant me grace to see the cross as the place of glory and joy. I love you, Amen.

13

Don't Forget Your Towel

John Chapter 13

Have you ever said "good-bye" to someone knowing it would be for the last time? Chapters 13 to 17 show Jesus preparing the disciples for his departure and their mission. We are now in the second act of John's Gospel. Up to now Jesus has been teaching and preaching to the crowds. From this point on he focuses on instructing his disciples because he knows he will soon leave them. Studying these instructions is so significant because they are found only in John's Gospel. One of the reasons we have four Gospels is that they each bring a different angle on Jesus and his teachings. Each of the Gospels makes us richer if we appreciate their differences and become familiar with them all. John's Gospel shows us perhaps the greatest intimacy between Jesus and his disciples. These chapters contain invaluable insights for modern-day disciples that open up to us the heart of Jesus as well as his mission and what each means for those who follow him.

The section begins with the extraordinary events of chapter 13. There may be nothing more radical Jesus ever did than what we see in this room. Let's open the door to a meal unlike any other in history.

Brothers in Arms

In the first twelve chapters of John, the disciples have been almost two-dimensional. They have been Jesus' helpers and pupils.

Now look at the change in the way Jesus talks to and refers to them. John describes himself and his fellow disciples as "his own" (13:1). Jesus calls them "little children" (13:33 NRSV), "friends" (15:15 and 21:4–5), "those whom you gave me" (17:6 and 9 NRSV), and "my brothers" (20:17).

The disciples have gone from being lowly helpers to partners in his ministry. This is also our status today in Christ. We are not add-ons to the Kingdom. We are full-fledged partners. How does that make you feel? Paul said we are "God's fellow workers" (1 Corinthians 3:9, 2 Corinthians 6:1). The writer to the Hebrews stated that we are brothers to Christ (Hebrews 2:11–18). John 13 demonstrates in Technicolor that Jesus thinks he is no more important than you or me. When you think of Jesus, are you afraid, intimidated or insecure? I am sure you've wondered, as I have, what it would be like to meet Jesus face to face. Would I be overawed? I am not completely sure, but, looking at the events of this chapter, I guess I would be more likely to be drawn to him than fearful of him. How can a man with a towel around his waist and a bowl in his hands stooping at your feet be any kind of negative threat? Isn't his initiative amazing?

Initiative Inertia

Some people were sitting around a table. A fire started in a wastepaper bin in the corner of the room. No one moved—everyone acted as if it wasn't there. The fire grew larger and more dangerous. If something wasn't done soon their lives could be in danger. Still no one moved a muscle. What one person in the group didn't know was that the others in the room were all actors. The whole thing had been set up as a psychological experiment into the effects of peer-pressure. The investigators wanted to see if the person who wasn't an actor would do something about the fire, or whether he would sit still.

Peer-pressure was so strong that the one non-actor was willing to allow all their lives to be endangered. What does it take to get us moving and serving? Why didn't the disciples take the initiative?

Perhaps there are two main reasons.

Cultural Complications

In the culture of Jesus' day a Gentile slave would have been expected to wash the feet. Such a distasteful action was beneath even a Jewish slave, and Rabbinic teaching said that they were not bound to carry out this duty. But it appears there is no such servant in this upper room. The disciples and Jesus are reclining around the table on couches (not on individual chairs). Their feet are off the floor, pointed outward from the table and quite near to each other. The climate is hot, the roads are dusty, and the feet are very, very smelly!

Dinner was already being served (13:2), the feet ought to have been washed long before. I fancy there was quite a bit of tension in the air. Everyone knew someone ought to step into the role of a servant, but no one wanted to make the first move. Who was it going to be? Certainly it shouldn't be Jesus. I imagine Peter looking at Andrew, James looking at Thomas, and everyone looking at John. Since he was probably the youngest, perhaps they thought he ought to be the one. It would have been unthinkable for a disciple of a Rabbi to wash someone's feet, let alone a Rabbi himself. But "Jesus stoops to perform a task that was considered too menial even for his disciples!"[1] How do you suppose the disciples felt as Jesus went around? I guess there was a convicted silence!

Perhaps you are in a situation where you don't feel it is your "place" to take initiative, but let's be like our Lord and serve anyway. Is there something you can do for someone? Do it. Don't wait for someone else. Do it today—do it now!

Who Is the Greatest?

The other reason I believe the disciples didn't get up and wash each other's feet was simply pride. Luke's account tells us that during this meal,

> A dispute arose among them as to which of them was considered to be greatest. Jesus said to them, "The kings of the Gentiles lord it over them; and those who exercise authority

1. Andreas Kostenberger, *Encountering John: The Gospel in Historical, Literary, and Theological Perspective* (Nashville: Baker Academic, 2002), 146.

over them call themselves Benefactors. But you are not to be like that. Instead, the greatest among you should be like the youngest, and the one who rules like the one who serves. For who is greater, the one who is at the table or the one who serves? Is it not the one who is at the table? But I am among you as one who serves." (Luke 22:24–27)

Could it be that while they are squabbling over who is the first-century Mohammed Ali, Jesus "got up from the meal, took off his outer clothing, and wrapped a towel around his waist" (13:4)? Imagine the stunned silence as Jesus rebukes, corrects and teaches them by his actions and words. How were they feeling after he asked them, "Do you understand what I have done for you?" (13:12). I guess I would be thinking something like, "You've exposed my pride!"

As I write this chapter I am sitting in the Red Brick Café in Wealdstone where I live (I often get more writing done when I am out of the house!). It is a café employing people with learning disabilities and training them for a career in catering. The trainers are engaged in a noble task. Many of the staff cannot read or write. Some are deaf and others have conditions that look like cerebral palsy and Down's syndrome. I like it here. The staff and I know each other and joke about the sofas here being more comfortable than the ones at home. But when I first came I didn't talk to them. Why? They looked different, they didn't speak clearly, they spilt my coffee into the saucer, they brought me the wrong cake, they were slow in fulfilling an order, they weren't friendly. I am ashamed of my pride. I judged them because they were different. I judged them without knowing their circumstances. I thought of them as less than myself. And me— a Christian!

How different from Jesus. He was from heaven and yet freely mingled with us. He reserved judgment and preferred to show grace. He loved all the men and women he met. There was no room for pride in him, and there is no room for pride in his followers. The bottom line of his command to his followers is to "love one another" with a new standard: "As I have loved you..." (13:34–35).

Let there be no prejudice and pride in our churches. Where this exists there is no Christ-like love, and where there is no Christ-like love there is no Christ. On the other hand, where such counter-cultural love exists, Christ is present, Christ is glorified and Christ changes lives, hearts and eternal destinies.

Counter-Cultural Love

Jesus expected his followers to love each other in the same way he had just demonstrated his love for them (13:34–35). He isn't expecting us to turn up at church with a bowl, soap and towel, but he is expecting us to practice a "weird," abnormal love for one another. To the world this will look very, very odd. Because we are his brothers and sisters, we are called to take the initiative in self-abasing love, seeking the good of our fellow brothers and sisters even to the extent that we go against cultural and social norms. The very nature of our faith is counter-cultural. If you have not grasped this yet, it is time to get used to it!

A few months ago the teenage son of a friend of mine was considering his baptism. Alex was convinced it was the right thing to do, but was hesitating. His father asked why. The answer was a common one for a child brought up in the church: "I don't want to conform to the expectations of the church. Everyone's expecting me to get baptized. I'm struggling with my desire to rebel against people's expectations."

His father made an excellent point by replying, "You've not got a choice about rebellion in general, only in its detail. You're going to rebel against either the expectations of people in the church or the expectations of people in the world. Now what sounds more fun? Rebelling against a few people in the church, or rebelling against the vast numbers of the majority of humanity in the world?" Rebelling against several billion rather than a few people sounded much more appealing to this young man, and he was baptized shortly afterwards.

Our call is summarized in 1 John 4:10–12:

> This is love: not that we loved God, but that he loved us and sent his Son as an atoning sacrifice for our sins. Dear friends, since God so loved us, we also ought to love one another. No one has ever seen God; but if we love one another, God lives in us and his love is made complete in us.

The challenge for us is deep. Bear in mind that Judas got his feet washed just like the rest of the disciples, but there was no appropriate response on his part. Reflect on this maxim: "Proximity does not guarantee intimacy." Judas had his feet washed by Jesus, but it did not change his heart. Judas ate together with Jesus, but it did not change his mind. Judas sat close enough to Jesus for him to reach over and pass him some bread (13:26), but it did not change his destiny. Judas is in the vicinity but not intimate. As soon as Judas takes the bread, Satan enters him, he goes out, and these ominous words are recorded by John: "And it was night" (13:30). John's entire Gospel hinges on this phrase. The one who was light and brought the light is entering a time of darkness.

This darkness overshadows the chapters that follow until the day of resurrection. In John 20:1 it says,

> Early on the first day of the week, while it was still dark, Mary Magdalene went to the tomb and saw that the stone had been removed from the entrance.

The darkness was about to be ended. Death had been destroyed, the power of sin overcome, and there would be no more night! In our world, in our lives and in our churches, the light we have is the light shed by Christ-like love. All our preaching, singing, praying, structuring, planning and fasting will be of no value unless we are a people of love—radical love, Christ-like love, world-changing, counter-cultural love. It is challenging to live up to this standard. Indeed, it is exhausting! That is why we need regular topping up (or filling up). This love is fed in our private devotional times with God and our fellowship with other disciples. Putting time aside to be with God and be with the church is not a "demand" but an opportunity to bask in, revel in, live in and fill up with the love of God. If we devote ourselves to this intimacy with Christ, we will experience and pass on the love that Jesus showed his disciples.

Who can you love in a "weird" way this week? Go on, I dare you, get out your towel and show some truly Christ-like love. When you go to church this coming Sunday, don't forget your notebook, don't forget your Bible, but whatever you do—don't forget your towel!

Questions for Reflection

1. What is the equivalent of the towel for you?
2. Who can you show some humble love to this week or even this day?
3. What can you do for them?
4. When will you do it?

Prayer

Father, thanks for the example of Jesus. I'm afraid of the sacrifice involved in loving like Jesus. It seems so costly. But he thought it was worth it, so please help me to think like he did. Give me the heart to love even when it looks weird. I trust you to take care of me. In Jesus' name, Amen.

14

Honeymoons and Cement Mixers

John Chapter 14

"Here's the deal," Jesus says to his disciples. "It's better for you if I clear off rather than stick around" (14:3 and 16:7, my rough translation!). This makes no sense to the disciples, but Jesus makes it clear: "I am going there...if I go...I will come back...I am going" (14:2–4). How can this be? Here is the miracle-working, word-of-God-speaking Messiah—the one prophesied about and longed for. All of Israel has been waiting in eager expectation for him to be revealed. Simeon proclaimed,

> "Sovereign Lord, as you have promised,
>   you now dismiss your servant in peace.
> For my eyes have seen your salvation,
>   which you have prepared in the sight of all people,
> a light for revelation to the Gentiles
>   and for glory to your people Israel." (Luke 2:29–32)

No wonder Joseph and Mary are amazed! Considering all this, surely it would be better for all concerned if Jesus remained here forever on the earth. Perhaps you feel the same. Wouldn't it have been better to live while Jesus was walking around? Well, according to Jesus the answer is "No"! John 14 tells us why.

Honeymoons and Cement Mixers

If you are married, do you remember your honeymoon? Ah,

how the eyes mist over and a rapt look emerges on the faces of married men and women! And don't think I am leaving you singles out. I was dreaming about my honeymoon long before I met my wife. I doubt things are different with you. While we were planning our wedding a wise man told me, "Spend as little as you can get away with on the wedding day and as much as you can possibly afford on the honeymoon. The wedding day passes in a flash, and you will remember almost nothing. The honeymoon lasts a week and you'll remember it forever!" How right he was. This isn't the place to recount all the details of our honeymoon. We spent a week in an idyllic forest-hidden whitewashed Welsh cottage nestling on the slopes of the picturesque Conwy Valley...(I am in danger of never finishing this chapter). Anyway, I'm sure we can all grasp the significance of those first few days together as a married couple.

It wasn't like that in the days of the New Testament. There was no lazing on the beach sipping cocktails, watching the golden sunset while holding your beloved's hand. In first-century Palestine when a son married he didn't leave home. It was common to build another room onto his father's house. He and his new bride would be attached to the family while having their own living space. In this way a central courtyard developed while an estate was constructed that grew into a large compound called an *insula* (*monai* in Greek). So in those days instead of tying old tin cans to the rear bumper of the getaway car and being waved off by tearful grandmothers as you exit stage left to your honeymoon holiday, your dad hands you a shovel and says, "Start mixing the cement, Son."

In some cultures this kind of practice continues if on a different level. My next-door neighbor moved to Ireland last month. His house is semi-detached (or a duplex in U.S. terminology). An Indian family owns the house attached to his, and they are buying Tom's house so that their son can live in it. Effectively the two dwellings have become one. While in Jesus' day it was rooms that were added one to another, my neighbors are adding a whole house to another to make, in a sense, one larger house. Whether you think this is oppressive or endearing, the truth is that this is a far more accurate picture of what Jesus is trying to convey in chapter 14. The western tendency is to equate maturity with independence and isolation.

So what is the significance of this for us? I have heard (and preached) quite a few sermons on this passage emphasizing the fact that there is a room ready for us. It usually goes something like this:

> "Never fear! No matter what happens to you in this life, all will be well in the next. Even though we may not have a place to 'lay our head' right now, there is a permanent place of rest prepared for us by Jesus in the life eternal."

This is true. But there is more in this image.

In My Father's House

Jesus *does* promise us a secure room in which to rest in the next life, but what is the *nature* of this room? We are not talking individual houses standing in three acres of fenced-off garden. Neither are we going to inherit a bolt-hole, a hiding-place, a panic-room or a sanctuary where we can shut out the world or anyone who might disturb us. I sense this is not the image Jesus had in mind. I suspect our own picture is strongly influenced by insecurity, introversion and western culture. We value individualism to a distorted degree.

Personal conviction is good. Taking *personal* responsibility for our faith and life is right (1 Timothy 4:16). But viewing isolated independence as a Christian virtue is not. We were not made to be *in*dependent, but *inter*dependent. I cannot imagine something that is not virtuous on earth becoming so in heaven. The room image positively tells us that we are personally cared for, loved by and provided for by Jesus, and that is a good thing (I will develop this below). But I am sure that Jesus also wanted us to see that each of these rooms is attached to the larger house that is his Father's ("In my Father's house are many rooms").

This image strengthens the teaching of Jesus that he wants not only to have a personal relationship with us, but at the same time he is building a community of believers (the church). If you live alone in a flat, it is possible to go through life with almost no interaction with others in the flats abutting your own. If you live in a stand-alone house on your own this will be even truer. But most of us have lived in family homes, or rented a room in a larger house, or spent time in a university residence hall. In such places you cannot help but interact with the other residents. In family homes you meet other members of the family at the dining table and in front of the TV. In house-shares you meet in the corridor and the queue for the bathroom. You meet when you've run out of milk or your neighbor has set his stereo to "stun" at 2:00 AM.[1]

Jesus is talking about intimacy. After the tenderness of his actions in John 13 (washing feet), a demonstration of the opposite of intimacy (betrayal by Judas), and teaching on the fuel of intimacy (loving like Jesus), we now find Jesus taking this teaching in new and surprising directions. Intimacy is a sign of a genuine follower of Jesus. But why is this? Because it is fundamental to the character of God. In the life to come he will bolt on additional rooms to his house so that we can be both near him *and* near one another.

How do you feel about this issue of intimacy? Are you the kind of person who revels in deep personal times with God but finds fellowship difficult? Or are you secure in a throng of people while fearing those times of quietness and solitude with the Lord? In my experience, most of us tend more to one side or the other. Neither is mutually exclusive of the other, and we can grow in our weaknesses. The key is to be honest about our fears and allow the Scriptures to teach, rebuke, correct and train us (2 Timothy 3:16–17).

---

1. I cannot resist an anecdote about my university days in halls. One weekend morning I was awakened at an ungodly hour by an alarm clock. It was not mine, but that of my friend Jon. His room was eight doors down the corridor. The alarm was a foghorn and was waking the entire corridor. He, however, continued to sleep through it all. I forced entry to his room, turned off the alarm, yelled at Jon (who was still asleep) and went back to bed. The enduring image from that morning is of a cup of cold black coffee rotating at 33rpm on the record turntable. It had clearly been going round all night. Ah! Student life! It will probably not surprise you to know that this young man became a consultant psychiatrist and is a leading figure in his profession.

It's Not What You Know, but Who You Know

The rest of chapter 14 develops the theme of our intimacy with God and Jesus. John 14:6 is one of the most famous passages in the Gospel: "I am the way and the truth and the life. No one comes to the Father except through me." It is a passage often used to prove Jesus is the only way to a saving relationship with God.[2] Fair enough. But does this do full justice to the passage? If I were Thomas or Philip, I think I'd be less focused on the word "except" and more focused on the words "I" and "me." He's telling them, "I will take care of you and all who follow me through you."

The emphasis is on knowing the Father and not on access to the Father (although both are included). As with many things in life, it is not *what* you know, but *who* you know that matters. The question each of us will face at the end of time is not "Did you know the right doctrine?" or even "Did you live the right doctrine?" Both are important questions, and we should strive to answer them with a confident yet humble "Yes!"[3] But I believe the question will be different. I think it will be, "Did you know *me*?"

The right doctrine and life are an expression of knowing God, but the point is to *know* God through Jesus. Why go on about this? Because it is all too easy to see becoming a Christian and living the Christian life as a matter of ticking boxes. As long as we have done what is necessary to get into the circle, we are safe. But crossing the line into the Kingdom isn't the point. Moving closer and closer to Jesus *is* the point. Here is a question for you: Are you closer to God now than when you started your Christian walk? As Gordon MacDonald puts it,

> The start of character transformation is movement toward the centre point of Christ. There is little if anything, in the concept of a circle that compels people to deepen in character. Once they are over the line and inside the circle, what does it profit to be concerned about the hidden life any longer?
> But if Jesus is the centre point, and he bids us come closer and closer, then there is incentive each day to reengage in

---

2. Along with Acts 4:12.
3. 1 Timothy 4:16, Luke 6:46, James 2:24, etc., all still apply.

increasing transformation. The closer we move to the centre, the more like the One at the centre we become. Moving closer—deliberately, strategically—becomes one's personal mission over the course of a lifetime.

...I feel as if I'm dealing with a fundamental misunderstanding in our perception of what it means to be biblical people. For too many of us, transformation consists of altering some behaviours, some vocabulary, some schedules, even some priorities. And we rejoice all too quickly when these alterations appear to happen. But the hidden life is far more important."[4]

I don't know how to do everything just right in the Christian life. But I do know what direction I need to go. Isn't that great? I love it when I can see the right direction. This is not rocket science. And a jolly good thing that is. Once I've got my orientation correct the only thing left for me to do is...what? John shows us repeatedly that the defining characteristic of Jesus' relationship with God was *love expressed in perfect obedience*. The best way John could think of communicating this was by quoting Jesus when he said, "the Father is in me, and I in the Father" (John 10:38). What was exclusive to the relationship between Jesus and the Father is now available for every disciple! It comes through the Spirit who could not be distributed until Jesus had been glorified. So *that* is why it is better for Jesus to go and the Spirit to come—then all can enjoy the intimacy that Jesus had with God!

Another healthy reason as to why it is better that Jesus is not physically around today is that it prevents an unhealthy focus on an individual. Some religions still insist on providing a figure-head, but it is not hard to see the dangers involved. The fact that he is available to all who receive the Spirit solves another problem. Think about it. How many of us could develop an intimate relationship with Jesus if he were still in the Middle East today?

The idea of the Father being "in" him and him being "in" the Father, of us being "in" the Father and being "in" him is fascinating. For an inspiring Bible study, why not look at the passages in John's Gospel about being "in"? For starters you could look at 6:56; 8:44;

---

4. Gordon MacDonald, *Mid-Course Correction* (Nashville: Nelson Books, 2000), 162.

14:10–11, 17; 17:21–23.[5]

This leads us to my favorite verse of the chapter, verse 23. Here it is:

Jesus replied, "If anyone loves me, he will obey my teaching. My Father will love him, and we will come to him and make our home with him."

That last phrase is also translated:

"...we will come to them and live with them." *(New Living)*
"...we will come to that man and make our home within him." *(J.B. Phillips)*
"...we will come unto him, and make our abode with him." *(KJV)*
"...we'll move right into the neighborhood!" *(The Message)*

What a privilege. What a joy! It was right for Jesus to leave because only then was he able to come in a new and deeper way. His departure meant his homecoming into my heart. Hallelujah!

Questions for Reflection

1. What does it mean to you that there is a room prepared for your personal use? Have you imagined it? How would it feel to live there in eternity?
2. If moving towards Jesus is our goal, what does that look like? How do you know whether you are going in the right direction?
3. Not only are we on our way to a room prepared for us, but we also must prepare room in our hearts for the Father, Jesus and the Holy Spirit to live in us. What preparation can you make so that God's stay is a pleasant one?

Prayer

Father, thank you that Jesus has prepared a room for me. I am so grateful to know where I'm going. Teach me to value this and be secure in this knowledge. Help me accept that I am not the builder of this room and I have not earned it. It is mine by grace. Give me

---

5. Other useful passages would include Jeremiah 31:33–34, Ezekiel 37:14 and 1 Peter 5:14.

the humility to open my heart to you. I want to welcome you in. Come in and make any alterations you see necessary. Beautify my heart as only you can. I trust you with the room of my heart. Fill it with your presence. Transform it by the power of your Spirit. In the name of Jesus, Amen.

15

God the Gardener

John Chapter 15

When I was fourteen years old, I was helping my father dig in the garden. He asked me what job I would like to do when I finished school. I said I wasn't sure. He suggested being a gardener. I thought he was mad! Out there in all types of weather digging?! My father said it would be healthy. I thought it sounded deadly.

It wasn't "cool" to be a gardener when I was a kid, but I am not so sure these days. Celebrity gardeners are on our TV screens all the time. Current shows in the UK include *City Gardener, Ground Force, Gardener's World, Garden Invaders, The Flying Gardener* and *The Green-Fingered Gardener from Guadeloupe* (okay, I made the last one up). Millions of people watch these shows. Suddenly gardening is "cool." Perhaps it is time for me to change my attitude towards being a gardener. However, there is a better reason to value gardening than the fact it is on TV. You see, God is a gardener (John 15:1)!

God Planted Israel in Canaan

> You brought a vine out of Egypt;
>   you drove out the nations and planted it.
> You cleared the ground for it,
>   and it took root and filled the land.
> The mountains were covered with its shade,
>   the mighty cedars with its branches.
> It sent out its boughs to the Sea,
>   its shoots as far as the River. (Psalm 80:8–11)

God promised Abraham a land for his descendants (Genesis 17:8). The Bible uses the image of God planting Israel in Canaan. The inheritors of this promise were put there to grow, flourish and bear fruit.

The house we lived in before our present one had no garden, but it did have a paved back yard. In that yard we had numerous pots and troughs containing raspberry bushes, roses, ivies, hostas and many other plants. We moved into our present home four years ago. This one has a proper garden. One of the first things we did was take these plants out of their temporary homes (the pots) and put them in the ground. It felt like setting the prisoners free! The plants had finally found a home. The people of Israel must have felt the same way when they finally settled in Canaan several hundred years after the promise to Abraham.

God Fed and Guarded the Vine

> In that day—
> "Sing about a fruitful vineyard:
>   I, the LORD, watch over it;
>   I water it continually.
> I guard it day and night
>   so that no one may harm it." (Isaiah 27:2–3)

God was a patient gardener taking care of the needs of the vine called "Israel." He fed it, he guarded it, he loved it. Some of the plants in our garden grow quickly (generally the weeds, it seems) and some grow slowly. In order to grow, all of them need feeding. Our compost waste is collected and spread on the garden to make sure the plants get the nutrients they need. Watering is generally not a problem in rainy London. I have not sung a song about our garden or talked to the trees, but perhaps I should if I really want to be like God.

Some plants are vulnerable to attack. When I was a kid we had an annual family ritual. It was called the "putting up the nets in the fruit cage to keep the birds off" ritual. It happened every Easter. My father and I went to the bottom of the garden to the location of the aluminum-framed tabernacle that was the fruit cage. Inside this cage were the holy raspberry, white currant, black currant and red currant bushes. My father and I lifted the nets-of-protection onto the frame and secured them in place with sacred twist-ties. The demonic birds of oblivion were prevented from stealing the righteous fruit for another season, and there was much joy in the land. But there was more in God's mind than simply preserving what he had gotten. The vines were fed and guarded for a purpose.

God Grew the Vine for Fruit

> In days to come Jacob will take root,
> Israel will bud and blossom
> and fill all the world with fruit. (Isaiah 27:6)

God always hoped the fruit to be borne on the Israel-vine would be a blessing to the world. Every plant has a function. Some produce edible fruit, some produce inedible fruit, some produce, in a sense, visual fruit in the form of leaves and beautiful flowers. The fruit, flowers and leaves are of many different shapes, colors and sizes, but the one thing that is common is that they all produce *something*. Plants that produce nothing are useless. Such plants may have been given time to produce, they may have been fed and watered, but in the end they are torn up and thrown away because they did not fulfill their purpose (Luke 13:6–9, John 15:6).

Sadly, God's patience was not always rewarded. Sometimes the plants he patiently tended produced nothing. At times God the gardener had to take drastic measures.

> I will sing for the one I love
> a song about his vineyard:
> My loved one had a vineyard
> on a fertile hillside.

He dug it up and cleared it of stones
    and planted it with the choicest vines.
He built a watchtower in it
    and cut out a winepress as well.
Then he looked for a crop of good grapes,
    but it yielded only bad fruit.

"Now you dwellers in Jerusalem and men of Judah,
    judge between me and my vineyard.
What more could have been done for my vineyard
    than I have done for it?
When I looked for good grapes,
    why did it yield only bad?
Now I will tell you
    what I am going to do to my vineyard:
I will take away its hedge,
    and it will be destroyed;
I will break down its wall,
    and it will be trampled.
I will make it a wasteland,
    neither pruned nor cultivated,
    and briers and thorns will grow there.
I will command the clouds
    not to rain on it."

The vineyard of the LORD Almighty
    is the house of Israel,
and the men of Judah
    are the garden of his delight.
And he looked for justice, but saw bloodshed;
    for righteousness, but heard cries of distress.
(Isaiah 5:1–7)

God Had a Plan

This all leads us to the radical impact of what Jesus says here in John chapter 15. Jesus tells us (drum roll, please) *he replaces Israel as God's vine.* By saying, "I am the true vine," he is telling his disciples not only that he will succeed where Israel failed, but also that this was what God had planned all along. Now not only will Jews enjoy the fruits of a relationship with God, but so will Gentiles, "All whom the Lord our God will call" (Acts 2:39), all who abide in Christ. Instead of being planted in the land of Israel, we are planted into Christ. Instead of God feeding, guarding and growing the people of God as a specific nation in a specific land, now it is in Jesus Christ we are fed and kept safe, and grow to become people of the new covenant (John 6:51, 10:28–29, 15:8).

This must have blown their circuits. It doesn't connect in quite the same way for us, but the following may help us get a better picture. When we understand the Old Testament images of the vine and vineyard, we get a much better idea of how radical and exciting this teaching of Jesus really is. As Jesus was talking, he may well have been standing in a vineyard. Not too far away was the temple. The disciples might have brought to mind the gold vine growing over the entrance to the Holy Place in the temple. This symbolized Israel. It was "growing" because wealthy Israelites brought gold tendrils, clusters of grapes or leaves, and these were added to the vine by the temple metal workers. Some clusters of grapes were as tall as an adult. Josephus says that when the Romans sacked Jerusalem, so much gold was taken away and ended up on the market that it depressed the price of gold in Syria by half![1]

Jesus is not using a cute gardening image. Instead, he is claiming to be the fulfillment of a promise made to Abraham—the father of the faithful. He is replacing, updating and perfecting the identity, character and nature of God's vine. He is the *true* vine. All people grafted into him belong to God. That's what is so exciting about this passage for me. It is so simple as to be brilliant! All I have to do is remain in Christ. I can do that. I may never understand all the complexities of the Trinity or predestination, but I can cling on to Christ. There are, however, a few challenges (aren't there always?).

Productive Pruning?

First, Jesus says something rather uncomfortable about pruning (15:2). It is amazing to think that even Jesus needed to be pruned. He had to be perfected (completed) for his purpose (Hebrews

---

1. Flavius Josephus, *War of the Jews*, Book 7, Chapter 4.

5:8–10). How much more I need pruning (Hebrews 12:4–13). Are you being pruned right now? As someone said, "If you're wondering where God is pruning you, ask yourself, 'Where does it hurt?'" It is easy to resent God's pruning, but reflect on this if you will: The most joyful Christians I know are usually the ones who have endured the most pruning.

Second, he says something about a bonfire (15:6). I love bonfires. At fourteen years old I was not too keen on digging (especially in the rain), but ask me to build a bonfire and I'd jump at the chance! What fun to pile up the wood, light the fire and then watch as voles, mice and hedgehogs ran for their lives from the towering inferno. I say I love bonfires, but that is when I am warming my hands on them on the non-burning side. I am not too keen to swap places with the hibernating hedgehog as it awakens early to find itself surrounded by the confusion of smoke, glowing embers and fierce heat.

This is a warning from Jesus, and a warning designed to insure against complacency. God is not looking to cast anyone aside, but just as the Israelites became complacent about their privileged position as God's chosen people (see the Isaiah 5 passage quoted earlier), we too can fail to keep our gratitude and first love (Revelation 2:4). So how do we guard against this?

What About Obedience?

I have spent a lot of time, coffee and headache pills trying to understand the obedience issue. Jesus clearly and unapologetically demands obedience. Obedience to Christ is essential. But we know that simply obeying the rules won't get you to heaven. There is a paradox between soul-killing legalism and soul-saving obedience.

So what is legalism? It is a word that gets bandied around with great abandon but less understanding. I suspect that if we asked a number of Christians what they think legalism to be, we would receive a very wide variety of answers. As far as I understand it, legalism is *not* "doing something out of a sense of duty" or "doing something despite the fact that we don't feel that our heart is in it."

If legalism *is* these things, then we are saying that we shouldn't pray if we don't feel like it. I am not suggesting we ignore our feelings, but simply that our behavior should not be controlled by them.

So what is legalism? I believe one way of defining legalism is:

believing and living as if you will be saved by "keeping the rules"

None of us will be saved by keeping the rules perfectly. It is not possible to keep them perfectly anyway! God has a different plan— it is called grace.

It is *not* legalistic to come to church when we don't feel spiritual.
It *is* legalistic to think that attendance at church gains us any special favor with God.

It is *not* legalistic to read the Bible when we feel distant from God.
It *is* legalistic to believe that by reading the Bible we are more likely to be loved by God.

It is *not* legalistic to share our faith with people when we are not sure we are doing it out of love.
It *is* legalistic to think that by sharing our faith we are more likely to be saved.

So back to John 15. Our obedience is essential; that is the command. But look at what comes after this command. Jesus talks about love, joy and friendship. Our obedience is an expression of love; love is the motivation. There is no contradiction between the two. In my garden some plants thrive, others die. If we remain in Jesus, we will be evergreen, ever-fragrant, and ever-growing. Let us be grateful that God is our gardener and that we are in his garden!

Questions for Reflection

1. Are you in the vine? Do you know how to be sure of this?
2. If you are in the vine, are you growing? In what area are you growing? What is your food?
3. If you are growing, are you producing fruit? Where is the fruit?
4. If you are producing fruit, is it lasting?

Prayer

Father, thank you I'm in the vine because Jesus grafted me in. Thanks for feeding me and keeping me safe. Help me to welcome your pruning and persevere through the pain so I can bear fruit that will last and bring you great glory. Help me obey you with the right spirit. In the name of Jesus, the True Vine, Amen.

16

Noddy and the Seal

John Chapter 16

What were you given when you left home—if anything? Some parents weep when their children fly the nest. Some rejoice! When I left for university my mother presented me with a yogurt maker (they were the in-thing at the time). Like all good mothers, my mum was concerned I might not eat properly. A little later I received a sandwich maker. The perfect combination for student life—yogurt to balance my bacteria and toasted sandwiches to warm my frozen body as I lay in my artist's heat-free garret (or attic-type space) contemplating the meaning of life and the complexities of Mozart's sonata form.[1]

When I left home I felt a giddy mix of fear and excitement. The first few months were a time of experimentation. It wasn't long before I was in a tailspin of despair and depression brought on by debt, drunkenness, the disappointment of failed exams, and being dumped by my girlfriend. For three weeks I sat in my room emerging only at meal and bar-opening times. I shall never forget the lifesaving conversation that brought me back to level ground. Finally I became desperate enough to ask for help (Luke 15:17) and called my mother. She gave me a listening, sympathetic, non-judgmental ear.[2] Both my parents offered love when condemnation was deserved. They removed confusion, relieved anxiety and restored hope.

---

1. The reality of my time as a music student was that I was pretty warm and comfortable most of the time! But, "Thanks, Mum." I ate a lot of yogurt and toasted cheese sandwiches.

2. My father also gave me excellent advice on money management (a story for another time).

As Jesus was about to leave his friends (14:2), I am sure he also had a mixture of feelings. He was very concerned for them. This was no cozy departure. It was to be the most traumatic parting of the ways imaginable.

Should I Stay or Should I Go?

Jesus knew he would not be with them on this earth much longer. He had been preparing them for his departure and now tells them how they can cope once he has left. Jesus tells them he will be giving them something much more sustaining, empowering and inspiring than a yogurt maker! He will be sending them the Holy Spirit! (v7). They will certainly need *something*. They have testing times ahead. Consider this lot:

- Difficult decisions (Acts 1:15–26)
- Imprisonment (Acts 4:3, 12:3–4)
- Opposition by authorities (Acts 4:18; 5:17–18, 40)
- Internal church crises (Acts 5:1–11, 6:1–6, 15:1–35)
- Martyrdoms (Acts 7:59–60, 12:1–2)

And you thought *your* church was going through a hard time? It was the Holy Spirit that guided and sustained them through all this and much more. I am tempted to think that if Jesus were to walk into my congregation next Sunday, his physical presence would make the challenges we face so much easier to handle. But he *is* present and *will* be there on Sunday and *every* day. Indeed, according to Jesus, we are better off with his spiritual presence than his physical presence. He tells the disciples, "It is for your good that I am going away" (v7). That must have been hard for them to believe. When we think that the spiritual presence of Jesus is some kind of second-best option, it betrays our lack of understanding about the Spirit.

What's the Fuss?

Can I ask you a question? When is the last time you read a book about the Holy Spirit? Here's the deal: Most Christian people I know (and I am including myself here) have read books on Jesus, but very few have read books about God or the Holy Spirit. Now I am all for reading a library full of books about the Christ. But is it right that we neglect the other, and rather significant, members of the Godhead? The Bible talks a lot about God and the Spirit. Do you? Yes, it is true some Christian movements glorify the Spirit to the extent that Jesus is shoved into the background. The Bible's portrayal of the Spirit makes it clear that the Spirit brings glory to Jesus, and any group or church that compromises this perspective is not in step with the Scriptures (16:14, 1 Corinthians 12–14).

However, most people I know tend to neglect the Spirit. Let's put this right. Why not pop along to your nearest Bible bookshop and buy a book on the Spirit, or order one from the Web?[3] We don't have time or space to do an in-depth study of the Spirit here, but let's at least consider some fuss-worthy aspects of the Spirit.

Noddy and the Spirit

The Spirit is given by Jesus (v7). Neglecting a gift given by Jesus doesn't seem like a great idea does it? The way we treat a gift tells us a lot about our relationship with the giver. On my desk stands an eggcup carved and painted to look like the PBS children's character "Noddy."[4] The eggcup is wooden, the paint has largely flaked off, and is of no monetary value. Yet it has a prominent position of honor where I see it every day. Why? Because my grandparents gave it to me forty years ago. I thought it had been lost until this year. My parents found it and gave it to me. I had not seen it for around thirty years, but when I held it in my hands a lump came to my throat. I recognized it immediately and remember many a childhood breakfast dipping bread soldiers into the runny yellow yolk. I can almost taste it now! Why is a faded wooden memento so significant? Because it may be the only thing I still possess that my Granny and Grandad gave me (they died more than twenty years ago). I will treasure it for as long as I live.

Do you treasure the Spirit given you by Jesus, or do you take him for granted? When is the last time you stopped to thank God for this gift? Why not offer a prayer of gratitude right now? "Father, I'm

---

3. You could try *The Spirit*, Douglas Jacoby (Spring, TX: IPI, 2005).
4. This site will give you an idea of what Noddy looks like: www.noddy.com

so grateful for the gift of the Spirit because…"

Satan and the Seal

The Spirit seals and guarantees our inheritance (Ephesians 1:13–14). What does this mean? Well, if you will forgive my fevered imagination, I'd like to tell you of something I have seen many times in my mind's eye. I rather fancy that every Thursday the Devil does a stock-take. His eyes range over the population of the earth to see who might soon be coming his way. He fixes his lustful gaze on a particular man or woman, and just as he is about to congratulate himself that fresh meat is sure to arrive in hell in the near future, there is a polite cough just behind his left shoulder. He turns round, and there, to his horror, stands Jesus.

"What are *you* doing here?!" the devil says, quaking with fear. "These are mine, *all* mine," he goes on, "and you can't have them. They're all sinners, 100% proof!"

"This I know," says Jesus, "but there's something you're forgetting. The sealed ones are mine."

"What gibberish are you spouting?" splutters the devil.

"You know what I'm talking about," says Jesus, "and there's no point arguing. The sealed ones are mine and they are safe. They are those who possess the Spirit I gave them at their baptism. It's not something magical. They're still sinners. They don't glow in the dark, and their individuality is intact, but they have a peace, a joy, a light in their eyes, a hope in their hearts, a faith in God and a love for the lost that the Spirit gave them. And more than that—they're slowly but surely, step by step, day by day, becoming more and more like…me!"

"I know, I know!" cries the devil. "It's horrible! Stop it, stop it!!"

And Jesus takes great delight in pointing out each and every sealed one to the devil, who by now wants to retreat to the comfort of hell (anywhere is more comfortable to the devil than being in the very presence of Jesus). "That one's mine," says Jesus, "and that one, and that one, and that one, and that one, and that one. Oh, and look, someone is being baptized, receiving the Spirit and their seal and guarantee right now in India, *and* Alaska, *and* Ghana, *and* China, *and* Lebanon, *and* Scotland, *and* Colombia, *and* Fiji, *and* Poland, *and* Cambodia, *and* Iraq, *and*...Satan? Satan? Where have you gone?"

Jesus looks around but the devil is nowhere to be seen. The archangel Michael has been observing all this while standing in the background. He moves to Jesus' side and they have a good chuckle. "See you next Thursday, Jesus!" he says and they go off to answer some prayers.

Do we have *any idea* of the power of the Spirit in keeping us safe from the devil's schemes? Why not say another prayer of gratitude? "Father, thank you for the sealing power of the Spirit because..."

God's Breath

The Spirit is often seen as God's "breath" (20:22). Here is a prayer-poem I read this morning. It encouraged me. Perhaps it will you, too.

Breath of God

Breath of God inspire us,
Renew our faith
Restore our vision
Revive our love.

Breath of God inspire us,
Replace our sorrow
Relieve our sins
Redeem our situation.

Breath of God inspire us,
Repair our brokenness
Recover our nakedness
Resurrect our deadness.

Breath of God come,
Refresh
Redeem
Restore us.[5]

Questions for Reflection

5. David Adam, *Tides and Seasons* (London: Triangle, 1989), 125. All rights reserved. Used by permission.

1. What does the gift of the Holy Spirit mean to you? Try to put it in your own words.
2. Have you ever made a list of what the Spirit does for you? Why not study what the Bible teaches about this and write down what you discover.
3. What difference will the Spirit make to your day (today) now that you've read and thought about John chapter 16?

Prayer

Father, thank you that Jesus gave the Spirit. Help me never take him for granted. Give me the eyes of faith to see what the Spirit is doing *for* me, *in* me, and *through* me. In the name of Jesus, the Spirit-Giver, Amen.

17

The 1-2-3 of Prayer

John Chapter 17

What is the most amazing prayer you have ever heard? In 1984 I was searching for a meaningful relationship with God. I went to a series of church meetings in Notting Hill (if you've seen the film of the same name, you'll know the area of London I'm talking about). I didn't see Hugh Grant or Julia Roberts, but I did see something more significant than a Hollywood star. I saw and heard a man pray like I had never heard before. At each service he was called forward to pray. He was a tall barrel-chested man with a deep, booming voice (rather like the actor Brian Blessed).

He didn't rush, but neither did he hesitate. He seemed *certain* God was listening to him. He gave the impression that God was very *real* to him. I sat in the balcony enthralled. I dared to open my eyes during the prayer convinced that an angel must be hugging him. I never got to know that man and I don't remember his name, but the experience remains vivid for me. I left those meetings impressed— but depressed. I was glad the barrel man was so sure God heard him, but I was more certain than ever God would never listen to my pathetic prayers.

I wonder how many of us today measure our prayers by the wrong standard? We've probably all heard someone pray in a way we feel we can never imitate. Who was it for you? A loving grandparent, a super-spiritual Sunday school teacher, a passionate missionary, a venerable elder? When we hear such people pray it is tempting to think they always prayed like that. Perhaps it is genetic? Why didn't God give me the auto-connect-with-God gene? Why do some people seem to have a wireless Bluetooth 8meg broadband connection to heaven when mine feels more like a 56k modem with dodgy software? It is so sad that I, and many like me, feel our prayers are inadequate when God has not told us any such thing. The problem is not so much where we start from in our prayer life or where we are right now, but whether we are learning.

We *can* learn how to pray. After all, Jesus had to teach his own disciples (Luke 11:1–13, 18:1–4), and they were people who had grown up in a religion and society that regarded prayer as normal (quite different from the experience of most of us today).

We can learn how to pray, but do we have the right model in mind? I fear that too many of us, myself included, have pictures in our heads that have more to do with forms of prayer affected by tradition and experience than by Jesus himself. What do you think about Jesus' prayers? His prayers are incredibly important. He prayed often (Luke 5:16), at length (Luke 6:12) and intensely (26:36–46).

At some point in writing this Gospel, John decided he wanted us to know how Jesus prayed. He must have had shed-loads of material to choose from. Therefore, the prayers of Jesus that *are* recorded should be especially important. The section we are looking at in chapter 17 is not a random globule of prayer. John chose it because it will help us understand something vital about Jesus and his message. It was written for you and me. We are being invited inside the prayer life of the Son of God—into the intimacy that is Jesus' relationship with God.

Jesus the Model

Jesus is about to go to the cross, his greatest test. John knows that unless we "hear" Jesus pray, we will miss something vital. If we focus exclusively on what Jesus did, we run the risk of missing why he did it and who he did it for. I sometimes wonder if the WWJD (What Would Jesus Do) bracelets don't create an unintentional problem. As noble and useful as their purpose may be, I rather think we need a different bracelet, one that has WWJT on it, standing for "What would Jesus *think*?" Isn't that more important than what he did? He did what he did because of how he *thought* about God and people. If we are going to imitate anything in Jesus (and indeed we should strive to imitate everything), then surely we must imitate the *how* and *why* and not just the *what*. In the context of this chapter, it is crucial to try and get inside the mind of the Messiah to see *how* and *why* he prayed. If we miss this we miss the heart of Jesus! Are you learning how to pray from Jesus? Have you read, studied, thought about and reflected upon his prayers? May I suggest you take some time to re-read chapter 17 and ask yourself the following questions?

1. Who would get the most glory if Jesus' prayers were answered?
2. How do you think Jesus was feeling as he prayed these prayers?
3. What do you think motivated him to pray these prayers?

Some of our answers are going to be speculative, but this does not mean the exercise isn't important. Too much of our Bible study can be academic when it needs to be more experiential (and I say this as one pursuing a degree in theology). Our prayers should be theologically correct, but they must also be, at least in part, an experience. Look at the Psalms! They are full of expressive angst, anger, fear, faith, judgment, joy, hype, hope, wonder and worship. Are your prayers an experience? Let's now look at the themes of Jesus' prayers in this chapter.

Worthless Worm or Precious Person?

Jesus was very secure in his identity. He knew he was God's Son (v1); he knew his role (v2); he knew what he had achieved and that he had pleased God with his work (v4). His prayer times confirmed his identity and strengthened him for God's work (a really encouraging study on prayer is to read the Gospel of Luke looking at Jesus praying and noting what happened *after* he prayed). When we don't connect with God in prayer, we forget who we are. We have been damaged by sin so that we don't see ourselves right. I often forget who I am in God's eyes.

Who or what do you feel like first thing in the morning? I certainly feel more like a worm than a man—until I meet with my God. Then I am reminded of how precious I am to him. A prayer connection with the Lord helps us remember who we are really intended to be. If Jesus benefited from reassurance (Luke 3:22), how much more do we need it? And this is personal. In terms of priorities it is not the church that needs to be more prayerful, it is you and me.

A few years ago a private jet went off course. Jet fighters were scrambling to intercept it. The pilots reported seeing the windows of the wayward jet frosted up. After flying in a straight line for several hours and at heights of up to 45,000 feet, the fuel ran out and 1999 U.S. Open Winner Payne Stewart's Lear jet crashed to the ground killing all aboard. Air traffic control knew something was wrong. The U.S. Air Force pilots knew something was wrong. But to the casual observer on the ground below everything looked normal. Anyone looking up into the sky would have been unaware of the impending tragedy and might have thought, "I wonder who that lucky person is traveling in their private jet?" The most likely explanation of the events was a rapid depressurization.[1] They died from lack of oxygen long before they hit the ground.

How do we avoid a "crash and burn" in our spiritual lives? Others may not be able to tell what is going on inside before it is too late. It is up to you and me to make sure we are breathing the spiritual oxygen provided by personal prayer. Jesus was able to endure to the end because he was devoted to his Father in prayer. We have that very same resource. Are we using it? Are you using it?

Difficult Disciples

Jesus prayed for his disciples. He loved them. He thought of them as his friends (15:15). The longest section of his prayer in this

---

1. www.airsafe.com/stewart.htm

chapter is for his disciples. It is as if he couldn't stop himself praying for them. Something poured out of him onto them. Have you ever found yourself praying for a friend and beginning to cry? There is an amazing connection that happens when we pray for people. I have often been more emotional in my prayers for people than I have been with them face-to-face. I don't really understand this, but I know that when I pray for my friends, I end up loving them more, being more sensitive to them, and being willing to make sacrifices for them.

Do you have difficulties with disciples? You know what I mean. Do you avoid certain people at church because they "rub you up the wrong way"? Don't you realize that these very people could become your best friends? Don't you see that they might be God's chosen instruments to help you grow?

At a recent church service we had a time of sharing about relationships. A brother shared how he and another disciple used to avoid a Christian called Sam because they thought he was arrogant. They got convicted about their judgmental attitudes and invited him to go on holiday with them. Once they were away and were forced to talk more deeply, they discovered Sam's great qualities. They came back from their holiday cemented as friends and have been inseparable ever since. I was really grateful for this brother's honesty. How many more of us need to act so courageously? Where do we find the courage? In prayer.

Think about it from Jesus' perspective. He had a hard time with this bunch of disciples! How on earth did he manage to carry on loving them through their faithlessness (Luke 8:25), pride (Mark 10:13–16, 35–45), arguing and stubborn spirit (Matthew 16:21–23), hot-headedness (Luke 9:51–56) and slowness (Matthew 16:9)? I would have given up on them long ago. What sustained his love? I believe at least part of it was the fact he had prayed for them all night before choosing them (Luke 6:12–16). He tells Peter that he is praying for him (Luke 22:32), and we can be sure that when Jesus "often withdrew to lonely places and prayed" (Luke 5:16) he must have been praying for his disciples. God makes no mistakes. He chose you and all the others in your fellowship. While we cannot be equally close to everyone, we can grow closer. Who are you praying for? Why not stop right now and take a minute to pray for someone?

Love and Glory

Unity is about love. Not structure. Maybe I am naïve, but it seems to me we can be unified with anyone if we love them. If they do not want to be unified with us, that is another matter. But unity with another disciple or disciples is always possible. This works if love is the foundation of our faith. Jesus came to this earth because he loved the Father. He loved his disciples for the same reason, and he died on the cross because of this amazing love (1 John 4:9–10). It is this love that motivated Jesus and is behind our love for each other (1 John 4:11–12). Although we struggle to be united because we offend one another, we can overcome such obstacles to unity because love covers a multitude of sins (1 Peter 4:8).

If you are struggling to be united with someone in the fellowship at the moment, may I suggest you read and meditate on Colossians 3:12–14? It is clear in this passage that we can be compassionate, kind, humble, gentle, patient and forgiving only because of love. Deep, intimate, brotherly love is the fertile soul in which unity grows.

But what is the motive for unity? Unity is not a "god." Much harm is done when we pursue unity as an end in itself. Conformity and forced agreement are the results. The motivation for pursuing unity is the glory it brings to God. In Old Testament times the "Glory" of God (*Shekinah*—his presence with his people) left the mountain (Exodus 19) to live in the tabernacle (Exodus 40:34–38). Later it left the tabernacle to live in the temple (1 Kings 8:10–11). John shows many times in his Gospel how Jesus replaces aspects of the old covenant. One of these is the temple. Jesus replaces the temple (John 2:19) and now the Glory resides in *him* (vv22, 24). *He* is the presence of God among his people.

In a most remarkable and unexpected turn of events, Jesus

makes it clear in this prayer that the glory of God is no longer to be restricted to one place or person. Jesus wants God's glory, his presence, to be in every disciple (v22). As they go out into the world, they will be taking the presence of God with them. This is part of the fulfillment of the prophecies about the new covenant (Jeremiah 31:31–34, Hebrews 8:7–13). So we see that God's glory, the mission of Jesus and the mission of his followers are all bound together. We are the temple (1 Corinthians 6:19, 2 Corinthians 6:16), and as we go into the world we, as those who have been touched and changed by God's glory, invite others to see, touch and experience this glory.

Among people who have walked this earth, the one who had the most powerful prayers was Jesus. Effectiveness in prayer is not a matter of volume, length or eloquence. I believe we can all have a powerful prayer life. Let us learn from Jesus by getting the 1-2-3 of prayer right: (1) praying to have a right view of ourselves, (2) praying for fellow disciples and, (3) praying for our mission, motivated by God's glory and fuelled by love.

Questions for Reflection

1. Are you a worm in your own eyes? If so, try praying through Psalm 8.
2. Which disciple do you pray for regularly? Choose one, and pray for him or her for a week.
3. Your temple has legs. Are you taking it for a walk? Take the glory of God and show it to the world today.

Prayer

Father, thank you for the example of prayer set by Jesus. Thank you that I don't have to compare myself with anyone else and that you like hearing me pray. Help me to grow in my prayer life as I pray for myself, my brothers and sisters, and those yet to be changed by your glory. Help me take your glory to the world. In the name of Jesus, and to your glory, Amen.

18

The Trials of God and Men

John Chapter 18

Celebrity trials grab our attention and the world's media. Even those of us not interested in Michael Jackson's music were curious about the result of his trial. People who had never heard of O. J. Simpson were gripped by the courtroom scenes. Whatever country or culture you are from, you will find high-profile legal cases selling newspapers and occupying the media's attention. I check out the BBC's Web site every day for news that interests me and there is, without fail, at least one headline involving a famous person and a court case.

But we are talking a whole different league with Jesus. No trial in human history has received as much attention as his. More has been written about it than any other. During the actual trial there were few that realized it was going on and perhaps none other than Jesus himself who understood its significance. But it turned out to be the most colossal case of injustice ever known. God had a plan, however, and he turned what was a tragic travesty into a total triumph. Let us spend some time today looking at the events and characters involved in this mega-trial.

Divine 'Docudrama'

This chapter plays out like a docudrama. Bear in mind that John was writing to people who probably already knew the story of what had happened to Jesus. He is not just relating facts but getting a point across. How does he do this? He switches the focus from character to character and location to location—I love the way John builds the tension. As we delve into this chapter I suggest you keep asking yourself, "So, what is the point John is trying to convey?"

I have no pithy stories or anecdotes to illustrate this chapter. I would like instead to invite you to enter the world of the text. Take the part of an "extra" in the docudrama; place yourself in the olive grove, at the door to the courtyard, in the house of the high priest, standing by the fire, outside Pilate's palace. What do you see, hear, and feel? Most importantly, what is it like to see what Jesus does and hear what he says? Aren't you drawn to the quiet dignity of this great, suffering, servant-king? Do you sense his security and godly confidence? And how about the characters surrounding Jesus? We are all in this chapter—somewhere or other—just look carefully in the shadows and you will see yourself.

John starts in the dark of the olive grove and introduces us to Judas guiding the soldiers. I can imagine them creeping through the undergrowth trying not to step on twigs. The scene becomes even more vivid as he mentions the torches, lanterns and weapons (v3). The drama increases as people fall to the ground (v6) and Peter swings his sword (v10). Jesus is shown in control as he "went out and asked them, 'Who do you want?'" (v4). Here is no cowering religious wimp. Jesus is strong, yet meek; courageous, yet humble as he steps forward to embrace his destiny: "Shall I not drink the cup the Father has given me?" (v11).

Soldiers then bound Jesus and took him to Annas, which is interesting in itself.[1] Have you noticed how the focus switches back and forth between different people and places? We go from the garden, to Annas, to Peter, back to Annas, back again to Peter and finally to Pilate. What is going on here? I can just see the first-century paparazzi trying to keep up.

---

1. Annas had been high priest, but the Romans deposed him in 15 AD. They installed his son-in-law, Caiaphas, instead, and he ruled from 18 AD–36 AD. So why was Jesus taken to Annas before Caiaphas? Most likely Annas still retained a great deal of influence and power. Perhaps he was seen by some as still being the "legitimate" high priest. As a matter of protocol Jesus is taken before Annas first in deference to his continuing power and stature. The other three Gospels tell us about the trial before Caiaphas which John omits here.

Contrasting Characters

John is showing us the dignity and legitimacy of Jesus in contrast to the indignity and illegitimacy of the behavior of those around him. Let me illustrate: Judas, the soldiers, the officials from the chief priests and Pharisees were creeping around in the dark—Jesus stepped forward to confront them. By his actions he was confronting their duplicity, for if they had had a legitimate case with which to arrest him, they should have done it in daylight in the city or at the temple. Why did they not do so? Because they did not have a good enough case.

Annas might have been seen as the legitimate high priest, but he did not deal with Jesus "legitimately." Neither did Pilate. Annas and Pilate did not conduct their trials legally. Annas as high priest asked questions about his disciples and teaching (v19), but according to the law he should first have presented witnesses to establish the accused person's guilt. Jesus was smacked in the face (v22) before anyone had produced actual testimony of his wrongdoing. What must Jesus have been feeling when asked, "Is this the way you answer the high priest?" (v22), knowing he himself was our "great high priest" (Hebrews 4:14). Indeed, he is a "merciful and faithful high priest in service to God" (Hebrews 2:17) in contrast to Annas who was neither merciful to him nor faithful to his God-given duty.

Annas was conducting this trial of Jesus in contradiction to the law *and* not recognizing the Lamb of God who had come "that he might take away our sins" (1 John 3:5, also John 1:29). If there was anyone in Jerusalem or perhaps on the entire planet who ought to have realized what was going on and the true identity and significance of Jesus, it was Annas as high priest. How tragic that the earthly, temporary high priest did not have his eyes open to the heavenly, permanent high priest.

Pilate fared no better. He did not bring actual charges against Jesus (v29). The Jews merely called him a criminal and asked to have him executed (vv30–31). Pilate said three times there was no basis for a charge against Jesus (v38; 19:4, 6; see also Luke 23:4, 14, 22).

No witnesses were ever produced, Jesus never actually stood trial, and the verdict in the case was obviously based on political convenience and not on factual evidence.

Irony is everywhere in these verses. Barabbas' name means "son of the father" (in Aramaic). He was the guilty man of violence who was released while Jesus, the true "Son of the Father" and the only innocent man on the earth, was condemned. Again, the contrast with Jesus is remarkable. Pilate was a ruler, but only as one under the ultimate authority of Caesar. As such he ought to have upheld law and justice. Jesus was a king (v37) and yet was under the ultimate authority of his Father while on this earth (John 5:19, 15:10). He did uphold his Father's will, even though it was about to cost him his life. He stood for justice for all people while a great injustice was being perpetrated upon him. He was willing to pay the ultimate price, while Pilate was displaying his true colors as a ruler of expediency.

But I have left someone out. This someone is terribly important.

Peter the Petrified

Annas was confused by religious pride and Pilate by political fears, but what about Peter? Ah, Peter—he is you and me. Let's face it, while I can be Annas and Pilate in different ways, it is Peter I relate to most easily. Yes, even the Peter in the garden lopping off the man's ear with a sword. What? Me, mild-mannered Malcolm? Yes, me, you and the rest of humankind! We are all capable of violence.

"No, not me!" I hear you cry. Are you sure? Given the right (or wrong) conditions and the right (or wrong) buttons being pressed, we all have our explosion point where loss of control is guaranteed. Righteous indignation and fits of rage can look remarkably similar. Some of us lose it frequently and publicly (Peter's pattern) while some of us lose it rarely and privately. Just a thought for the natural Peters among us: Are you known as a person of self-control or do people reach for fire extinguishers when you open your mouth? (See James 3:5–6.)

And what of Peter at the door to the courtyard warming himself by the fire? It is not a huge distance from warrior to weakest link. The contrast with Jesus is, again, stark. Jesus was in control in Gethsemane, while Peter was out of control. Jesus was dignified and restrained, while Peter was impetuous. Under arrest Jesus confronted his accusers with truth (vv20ff), while Peter sought to retain his freedom by avoiding telling the truth to his inquisitors. Jesus was testifying to the truth; Peter was running from the truth. Jesus challenged his accusers to specify if he had told lies (v23); Peter told lies to protect himself. What does it take to get you to compromise your Christian beliefs or ethics? Our friend Pete had forgotten what Jesus said in the Sermon on the Mount:

> "Blessed are those who are persecuted because of right-
> eousness,
> for theirs is the kingdom of heaven.

> "Blessed are you when people insult you, persecute you and
> falsely say all kinds of evil against you because of me. Rejoice
> and be glad, because great is your reward in heaven, for in
> the same way they persecuted the prophets who were before
> you." (Matthew 5:10–12)

Of course we know that Peter changed, but we are getting ahead of ourselves. That will have to wait until chapter 21. For now, perhaps this is a time to reflect on what conditions tempt us to compromise. Is it pressure from a boss at work? Can you resist family force? Are you easily bullied by neighbors?

We see a succession of characters contrasted with Jesus. We can learn several lessons about ourselves from Peter, Judas, Annas and Pilate. The *main* thing however, is to see them in sharp contrast to Jesus. In this chapter he is the most humble, most righteous, most obedient and, somehow, most free and secure. He is the only one in the entire chapter at peace—yet he has the most to lose. What an irony and what an example for us to follow! The way to security and freedom is not in insisting on our rights or retaining control over our destiny, but in having the faithful courage to surrender to God's will and follow the model of Jesus Christ. Who is *really* on trial here? Is it Jesus? Or is it Judas (those who betray), Peter (those who follow but fail), Annas (the religious establishment) or Pilate (the political authorities)?

Here is the question: who are you like right now? Who do you *want* to be like today? Do you want to be like Judas who did what was right so long as Jesus matched his agenda? Do you want to imitate Pilate who does what is right so long as his career isn't compromised? Do you want to be like Annas who is prepared to be religious so long as no one challenges his interpretation? Do you want to be like Peter who is courageous as long as it is about swords and not about loyalties? I know there is a lot of Judas, Peter, Pilate and Annas in me. Judas twisted the point. Annas missed the point. Pilate ignored the point. Peter forgot the point. *We mustn't twist it, miss it, ignore it or forget it.*

What is the point? It is all about Jesus. This docudrama is about Jesus. Our faith is about Jesus. The gospel and the cross are about Jesus. Our lives are about Jesus. Never forget this.

Questions for Reflection
1. Who do you identify with most in this chapter? Why?
2. What do you think you would have done in Peter's sandals?
3. Do you think I've got the right emphasis in this chapter? Is it possible John's point is less about Jesus (he doesn't speak all that much, in fact) and more about the "supporting" characters?

Prayer
Father, thank you for the dignity, strength and spiritual courage of Jesus. Help me to see whether I'm more like Judas, Annas, Peter or Pilate. I want to be more like Jesus, but I feel much more like the other characters in this chapter. Help me, Father, to learn and grow. Give me strength to drink my cup, speak the truth and not shrink from persecution that comes from righteous living. In Jesus' name, Amen.

19

The Book of the Film

John Chapter 19

Films are the story-telling medium of our time. They are a window onto our societies' priorities, fears and dreams. What do we see when we look through the Hollywood window?[1] We observe a world where temptation is an industry. We see a message saying, "Give in to temptation. Is sex available? Take it. Has someone hurt a person you love? Take revenge. Have you been mistreated? Then your bitterness is justified and should be indulged."

Given this, isn't it amazing that the film *The Passion of the Christ* did so well at the box office? It is a movie that doesn't glorify or glamorize wealth, ambition, sex or revenge. Such a counter-Hollywood-values message runs at right angles to the norms of entertainment expectations. The fact that Mel Gibson is a devoted Catholic, a huge movie star, spent ten years getting the film made, and invested around £14 million (around 27 million U.S. dollars) of his own money in the project is impressive. But this doesn't explain the vast numbers of people who have been to see it. Many in the cinema audiences were people of the Christian faith, but many were not. Two thousand years after the event people are still drawn to the cross, that "emblem of suffering and shame."[2]

Why does the death of a wandering Jewish preacher two millennia ago stand out in human history? As we study through John chapter 19, I'd like to ask you to keep this question in the back of your mind:

---

1. I'm not anti-Hollywood, by the way. My points apply to Bollywood, French, and British films, and all other secular film foundations.
2. George Bernard, "The Old Rugged Cross."

What is it that makes this man's death so different from that of anyone else?

Saving or Shaming?

Pilate seems to be very conflicted (to use the modern jargon). He knows Jesus is innocent, but caves in to the crowd with a cynical disregard for justice and truth. Jesus however, even though he is the victim of unprecedented injustice, displays compassion in submitting to the cross for our sake (Romans 5:8, 2 Corinthians 5:21). Injustice is a terrible thing to bear when you are the victim. I suspect that most of us can think of a time when we were unjustly accused and unable to prove our innocence. Why not revisit that time now in your mind? How did you feel? Keeping this in mind will help you appreciate better what is going on in this scene.

The chief priests were sure their country would be better off with Jesus dead (John 18:14). They thought he was shaming their country and religion (or, at least, their traditions). Little did they realize that killing Jesus was just another example of Israelite leaders silencing the man of God sent by him to save his people. As Jesus said in Luke 13:33–34,

> "...surely no prophet can die outside Jerusalem! O Jerusalem, Jerusalem, you who kill the prophets and stoned those sent to you, how often I have longed to gather your children together, as a hen gathers her chicks under her wings, but you were not willing!"

When Jesus enters Jerusalem, he weeps because he can see what is coming:

> "If you, even you, had only known on this day what would bring you peace—but now it is hidden from your eyes. The days will come upon you when your enemies will build an embankment against you and encircle you and hem you in on every side. They will dash you to the ground, you and the children within your walls. They will not leave one stone on another, *because you did not recognize the time of God's coming to you*." (Luke 19:42–44, emphasis mine)

How ironic, no, how *tragic* that the high priests and their officials were blind to this. They not only could not see the impending doom, they hastened its arrival! Jesus was not shaming their nation or their religion—he was saving and fulfilling their purpose.

Long Live the King—Which King?

The chief priests deny Jesus' sovereignty by saying, "We have no king but Caesar" (v15) and "Do not write 'The King of the Jews,' but that this man claimed to be king of the Jews" (v21). Instead they proclaim a pagan ruler to be their king. What an indictment of their lack of loyalty to God. Way back in their history the Israelites said to Samuel, "…now appoint a king to lead us, such as all the other nations have" (1 Samuel 8:4). Samuel was not impressed and consulted the Lord. God told him, "It is not you they have rejected, but they have rejected me as their king" (v7).

John chapter 19 brings the centuries of God-as-King-rejection to its inevitable wretched climax. The chief priests proclaim, in the presence of the Messiah, their long-awaited King and Son of God, that they would rather serve a pagan Gentile king than the one sent from heaven to redeem his people (John 6:38–40, Titus 2:11–14).

Jesus knew this was coming when he told the Parable of the Tenants in Luke 20:9–19. He describes how the landlord (God) sent several servants (prophets) to the vineyard (Israel) to collect what he was due (honor, respect, worship, love, obedience), but they were beaten up and sent away with nothing. Finally, God says, "What shall I do? I will send my son, whom I love; perhaps they will respect him" (v13). The Israelites kill the son, however, and Jesus tells them what God will do with the rebellious murderers: "He will come and kill those tenants and give the vineyard to others" (v16). The crowd cannot believe this, but,

> Jesus looked directly at them and asked, "Then what is the meaning of that which is written: 'The stone the builders rejected has become the capstone'? Everyone who falls on that stone will be broken to pieces, but he on whom it falls will be crushed." (Luke 20:17–18)

The rejected capstone is Jesus, and those who refuse to be broken upon him are those who are too proud to admit their spiritual barrenness (Isaiah 66:2, Matthew 5:3, Luke 18:9–14). As a result, the chief priests are soon to be crushed—a process that begins with the resurrection and concludes with the destruction of Jerusalem and the temple in 70 AD. No wonder, then, the daytime-darkness, curtain-tearing, earthquake and tomb-raisings (Matthew 27:45–53). I am amazed the whole of creation didn't just fold in upon itself! The question we might consider is this: are we honoring the Son? Does he define truth of doctrine and practice for our lives? Are we blinded by tradition or the temptation of retaining the comfort of the status quo?

Silent Trust

Now here is the point that gets me; here is the thing that makes me stand up, shut up and go goggle-eyed: Jesus takes it on the chin and says *nothing* in his defense. He limits himself to a few short phrases. In John's Gospel we find recorded just the one statement of truth about power and authority to Pilate (that, I think, may have been designed to get Pilate thinking about truth, v37), a few words of comfort to his mother and to John (vv26–27), an expression of human need (v28) and a declaration of finality (v30).

Pilate, Herod and the Jewish religious and legal authorities looked after themselves. Jesus looked after others. His silence spoke louder than their false arguments. God must have longed to save his Son from this agony, but his desire to rescue Jesus (the sinless) was overcome by his desire to save us (the sinners). Jesus' desire to rescue me overcame his desire to be rescued. He gave me his life jacket, his place in the lifeboat, his parachute, his last tank of air. He gave it to me, a spiritual criminal, knowing that he would be condemned in my place.

How and why could he do this? Well, one of the most powerful statements of the cross is that we are to trust God for justice. Jesus was cheated out of justice at the hand of humankind, but he received justice later at the hand of God. He trusted that the future "joy" (Hebrews 12:2) would make the present pain a price worth paying.

This trust was possible because he was secure within the love of God. Isn't this one of our greatest challenges? We struggle to trust God with patience under suffering because we struggle with being secure within the love of God. Jesus is our example (1 Peter 2:21–25), and we can take inspiration from him. If he suffered such terrible injustice and yet was vindicated by God, then we can expect the same thing—even if in the next life and not this.

This powerful trust leads to victory. Finally Jesus is able to say, "It is finished" (v30). Most of us will have no choice as to when we will die, but Jesus was in control of that moment. His spirit was not torn away from him, demanded of him or stolen from him. He gave it up. He said, "Take it; it is yours, my Father." He gave it into his Father's hands (Luke 23:46) to do with whatever he wished. He knew that God would unleash all the punishments of hell upon his spirit. He knew that his Father would be nowhere to be seen, heard or felt—at least for a while. That "while" must have felt like eternity. Heaven and hell met at the cross, and Jesus experienced all of sin's power. No wonder the crucifixion still fascinates so many even today. This was a titanic struggle of greater proportions than ever seen before or since.

Warning and Welcome

A famous preacher said,

> The most terrible warning to impenitent men in all the world is the death of Christ. For if God spared not his own son on whom was only laid imputed[3] sin, will he spare sinners whose sins are actual and their own?[4]

We have been warned. Without Christ we will pay for our sins. But there is more. It turns out that this film's genre is not tragedy or horror. It is a love story. One day Jesus visited a man. Jesus said, "I love you." The man said "How much?" Jesus lifted his arms and spread them wide in the shape of the cross and said, "This much!" The cross is God's ultimate expression of love. As such, we will do

---

3. "Imputed" here means given rather than earned. In other words, Jesus suffered because of others' sins and not his own (he was sinless).

4. Charles Spurgeon from his sermon, "Why Should I Weep?" delivered October 22, 1876, at Metropolitan Tabernacle, London.

well to reflect on the cross as often as possible. This purifies our motives, opens our hearts and confirms our hope of eternity. To the God-of-the-cross be the glory!

Questions for Reflection

1. Have you been "broken," or are you in danger of being "crushed"? How can you be sure of spiritual insight into your spiritual condition?
2. How meaningful is the average communion for you? Is there anything about this chapter that could deepen your appreciation of the Lord's Supper?
3. Is the cross mainly a sign of suffering or victory for you? Can you hold these twin themes together?

Prayer

Father, words cannot express the awe I feel towards Jesus. I want him to be my King—now and always. Sometimes I find it hard to trust you when I'm suffering. Please give me faith like Jesus to persevere and live in hope. In his name, Amen.

20

Resurrection Restoration

John Chapter 20

What is the resurrection all about? Why does it mystify and fascinate? Has any event in human history provoked more controversy, ridicule, faith and hope? Before we move on to the meaning of this chapter for us, we must pause to consider the nature of the facts we are dealing with.

The Skeptics

Believe it or not, there are even Bible-believing people who don't believe in the bodily resurrection of Jesus Christ. As John Wenham says,

> Though the resurrection of Jesus has been the fundamental tenet of the Christian faith from its beginning, this tenet (sad to say) has been abandoned in recent years by many would-be Christian leaders. This includes a number of distinguished Anglican scholars who have either denied the bodily resurrection (e.g. the late Professor G.W.H. Lampe) or treated it as unimportant (e.g. Bishop J.A.T. Robinson) or declared its written records to be hopelessly contradictory (e.g., Professor C.F. Evans).[1]

So we see that the problem of unbelief is not just amongst atheists or agnostics, but even those who claim to be of the faith of the apostles. We must decide who to listen to for the evidence. A theologian called Rudolf Bultmann said, "If the bones of the dead Jesus

---

1. John Wenham, *Easter Enigma* (Eugene, Oregon: Wipf & Stock Publishers), 11.

were discovered tomorrow in a Palestinian tomb, all the essentials of Christianity would remain unchanged."[2] Is this true?

Is It Important?

Have you ever looked at the content of the sermons in the book of Acts? It makes a fascinating study that I would thoroughly recommend. Every New Testament sermon is centered on the resurrection. This isn't what I expected when I started to investigate what the apostles and other early disciples preached.

The early Christians clearly believed the resurrection was the central plank of their message. Without it the rest would fall. Paul was certain it happened. The skeptics are not. We must be sure what we believe.

> And if Christ has not been raised, our preaching is useless and so is your faith. More than that, we are then found to be false witnesses about God, for we have testified about God that he raised Christ from the dead. But he did not raise him if in fact the dead are not raised. For if the dead are not raised, then Christ has not been raised either. And if Christ has not been raised, your faith is futile; you are still in your sins. Then those also who have fallen asleep in Christ are lost. If only for this life we have hope in Christ, we are to be pitied more than all men. (1 Corinthians 15:14–19)

A secular author says:

> Now who is more likely to know what Christianity is, what its essentials are and whether these essentials would remain unchanged if Christ's corpse were to turn up tomorrow—the apostle or the sceptic? One of the religion's first-century founders or one of its twentieth-century subverters? A Jew who knew Christ or a German scholar [Rudolph Bultmann] who knew books?[3]

Who will we listen to—Rudolph or Paul?

---

2. Peter Kreeft and Ronald K. Tacelli, *Handbook of Christian Apologetics* (Downers Grove, Illinois: InterVarsity Press, 1994), 176.

3. Ibid, 177.

The Scriptures

When Paul wrote 1 Corinthians (around 55 AD) there were many people alive, including most of the apostles and early disciples, who had witnessed the risen Lord. He writes,

> For what I received I passed on to you as of first importance: that Christ died for our sins according to the Scriptures, that he was buried, that he was raised on the third day according to the Scriptures, and that he appeared to Peter, and then to the Twelve. After that, he appeared to more than five hundred of the brothers at the same time, most of whom are still living, though some have fallen asleep. Then he appeared to James, then to all the apostles, and last of all he appeared to me also, as to one abnormally born. If there is no resurrection of the dead, then not even Christ has been raised. And if Christ has not been raised, our preaching is useless and so is your faith. More than that, we are then found to be false witnesses about God, for we have testified about God that he raised Christ from the dead. ...And if Christ has not been raised, your faith is futile; you are still in your sins. (1 Corinthians 15:3–8)

From this we can see that the resurrection is vital to our faith and hope. There are many other passages showing that the Bible authors believed in a risen Jesus, but space forbids a detailed study. However, if you have never looked at this topic in the Bible, please make it a priority. Along with studying the Bible, also read what others have written about the resurrection.

Good Books

How many books on the resurrection exist? Countless numbers, I'm sure! I have got a few on my bookshelves: *Who Moved the Stone?* (Frank Morrison), *The Resurrection Factor* (Josh McDowell), *Easter Enigma* (John Wenham), as well as sections in *Reasons for Belief* (John Oakes), *More Than a Carpenter* and *Evidence That Demands a Verdict* (Josh McDowell), *The Case for Christ* (Lee Strobel), *Handbook of Christian Apologetics* (Kreeft and Tacelli), and *True and Reasonable*

(Douglas Jacoby), not to mention numerous articles in Bible encyclopedias and the like. Have you read a book about the resurrection? It will strengthen your faith and help you explain it to others. If you know a good book, please tell me and share it with others. Josh McDowell said,

> The early success of the Christian church is an historical phenomenon that must be explained…. It thrived in the very city where Jesus was crucified and buried. Do you believe for a moment that the early church could have survived for a week in its hostile surroundings if Jesus Christ had not been raised from the dead?… Dr Daniel Fuller observes that "to try to explain this (the church) without reference to the resurrection is as hopeless as trying to explain Roman history without reference to Julius Caesar."[4]

When compared to the Scriptures, books have limited use, but they have given me many useful insights that I had missed in my own study. Why not pop out to your local Christian bookshop or visit an Internet site and buy a book on the resurrection today?

Having spent a little time confirming the significance of the resurrection, now let's turn to the people involved in chapter 20.

Expect the Unexpected

After three years with Jesus, the disciples must have gotten used to expecting the unexpected! Barely a day seemed to go by without Jesus redefining their understanding of the law, challenging their assumptions about God's priorities, or giving the Pharisees a hard time over something that everyone thought was sacred. He spoke well of Samaritans, touched a leper, said he predates Abraham, and talked about replacing the temple. Strange goings-on indeed! And he is not finished yet. The resurrection appearances continued this theme.

Women As Witnesses

God loves to do things differently, at least different from the way society thinks would be right. In the Ancient Near East women were

---

4. Josh McDowell, *Resurrection Factor* (Nashville: Thomas Nelson, 1993), 129.

not regarded as legitimate legal witnesses. But who is the first witness to the empty tomb? Who is first to have a chat with the risen Jesus? Who is the person he chooses to pass on his instruction to the apostles? A woman—and one with an extraordinary demon-possessed past (Luke 8:2)! Perhaps this reminds us that we are all equal in the sight of God. Certainly it tells us that no matter our background or how society views us, we are all called to be and are capable of being valid witnesses to the good news of the resurrection.

Do you struggle to believe that God wants to use you as a witness? Do you struggle to believe you *can* be an effective witness? If no other passage spells it out, then this one does. If God chose Mary Magdalene as the *first* witness when it would have made more sense to have chosen Peter, James, John, the chief priest ("See, I told you I was who I said I was!") or even Nicodemus or Pilate ("Big mistake releasing Barabbas. And doing the hand-washing thing isn't going "wash" with my Father in heaven, by the way!"), then there has to be a reason. What screams at me is this: God *loves* the little guy. God loves to *use* the little guy (and gal). So we are all okay with God and we are all useful to God.

That means you, too—yes, you—the one I am talking to right now. Stop what you are doing. Stop what you are thinking and say after me,

God loves Malcolm (put your own name here).

God can use Malcolm (your own name again).

Keep praying it until you believe it—because it is true.

A Baffling Body

Work this one out: Jesus had a body that could be "clasped" (Matthew 28:9) and touched (John 20:27), and that got hungry and could eat fish (Luke 24:41–43). But his body could also walk through locked doors (John 20:19, 26) and vanish from sight (Luke 24:31)! He was not recognizable on some occasions (Luke 24:16,

John 20:14), but was very clearly Jesus at other times (John 20:28, 21:7). Hmm. Something is going on here. Why do John and the other Gospel writers record these apparently contradictory facts? We already know Jesus does miracles (walking on water, instant healings, etc.), but the concentration of weird abilities in the post-resurrection accounts seems deliberate to me. Why so much detail in such a small section of scripture? What is God trying to get across? Is he telling us something about what our existence will be like after our own death and resurrection? Jesus is the "firstborn from among the dead" (Colossians 1:18) and "we shall be like him" (1 John 3:2) when we join him in the next life. Paul tells us that we will have bodies in the life to come, but that they will be different:

> So will it be with the resurrection of the dead. The body that is sown is perishable, it is raised imperishable; it is sown in dishonor, it is raised in glory; it is sown in weakness, it is raised in power; it is sown a natural body, it is raised a spiritual body. (1 Corinthians 15:42–44)

He goes on to say,

> And just as we have borne the likeness of the earthly man, so shall we bear the likeness of the man from heaven.
> I declare to you, brothers, that flesh and blood cannot inherit the kingdom of God, nor does the perishable inherit the imperishable. Listen, I tell you a mystery: We will not all sleep, but we will all be changed—in a flash, in the twinkling of an eye, at the last trumpet. For the trumpet will sound, the dead will be raised imperishable, and we will be changed. For the perishable must clothe itself with the imperishable, and the mortal with immortality. When the perishable has been clothed with the imperishable, and the mortal with immortality, then the saying that is written will come true: "Death has been swallowed up in victory." (1 Corinthians 15:49–54)

What kind of body does this conjure up in your mind? Are you any the wiser? It is common for the Bible to give us glimpses of things that are outside our ability to completely comprehend. I don't know what my post-death/resurrection body will look like exactly, but I am pretty sure you will recognize me and I will recognize you. Another thing I am sure of is that I am going to be like Jesus in a purer, more complete way than I can imagine (I am looking forward to that!). This is guaranteed by two things,

1. Jesus' victory over death and the grave
   (1 Corinthians 15:55–57)

and

2. My participation in that victory through baptism
   (Romans 6:3–5).

Now that is good news worth sharing!

Restoring Relationships

So much of Christian apologetics regarding the resurrection focuses on giving evidence for its historicity that we've often missed the sheer beauty of these passages. The magic of John 20 and 21 is the theme of restoration—a combination of the miraculous restoration of Jesus to life and his restoration of relationships. Jesus comforts Mary (20:11–17), his disciples (20:19–22), Thomas (20:27), and we will see him restoring Peter in chapter 21. Perhaps our reading should focus less on the slowness of the disciples to believe or Thomas' failure to be at "church," and more on the passionate desire of Jesus to reassure, restore and remind.

He wants them to have faith. He wants them to know his love. He wants them to believe he is always with them. He has to return to them, not because it makes his resurrection any more real, but because he is compelled by his love for them. The last time he had seen them their faces were etched with fear, disbelief and grief. This might be a little irreverent, but I rather fancy that one of the reasons

Jesus appeared to them was, at least in part, just to see the look on their faces! Jesus loved to put wrong things right.

Are there any relationships you need to put right? Are there any people you can help to be reconciled either with each other or with their God? That's what it is all about. Anyway, more on this in chapter 21. See you there.

Questions for Reflection

1. Are you confident in defending the facts of the resurrection? What can you do to become better informed and prepared?
2. In what way is the resurrection relevant to your life day to day?
3. Whom do you identify with most in this chapter? Mary, the disciples, Thomas or Jesus? Why?

Prayer

Father, thank you for exercising your power to raise Jesus from the dead. Banish from my heart any fear of sin or death. Give me the heart of Jesus to strengthen the faith of others. Help me to be one who restores relationships, and guide me to those who want to be reconnected with you. In the name of the resurrected Jesus, Amen.

21

Memorable Meals

John Chapter 21

What is your most memorable meal? Was it with someone famous, or perhaps a special wedding anniversary or birthday? Maybe it was a really expensive meal. Some of my most memorable meals include the following: my eighteenth birthday when my parents cooked and served a superb *daub de boeuf* for me and seventeen of my friends, the first meal Penny and I ate together in a dingy Indian restaurant in Birmingham before we were going steady,[1] the meal I cooked for the two of us on our honeymoon when I cried for joy that God had blessed me so much with an incredible wife, the meal in India that caused me much pain in my digestive system, the very expensive restaurant we took my parents to in order to celebrate their fortieth wedding anniversary that caused me much pain in my wallet.

Jesus had many memorable meals with people.[2] Probably none were as memorable for Peter as this breakfast barbecue on the seashore. It is a great story, but why was *this* meal so important?

Slowly Sinking In

I don't know about you, but sometimes I don't get things first time round. It took my poor wife ten years to help me see the significance of budgeting. Now I am a convert. Jesus wanted things to sink

---

1. The Dilshad International in Selly Oak, otherwise known by generations of students as the "Dingy Dilshad" due to the low lighting designed, in our opinion, to hide the true state of the shabby décor!

2. Conrad Gempf has written an excellent book along this theme called *Mealtime Habits of the Messiah* (Grand Rapids: Zondervan, 2005).

in to his disciples, so he patiently came back to them time and again after his resurrection.

This fishing trip marks their third post-resurrection chat. Just seven of the disciples were on hand (is there some significance in the number seven, it being the number of perfection?). Perhaps they were the opinion leaders. Certainly James, John and Peter were three of the most "character-full" of the apostles, constituting the inner three often taken aside by Jesus (Matthew 26:37, Mark 5:37, Luke 9:28). They had all been commissioned in John 20:21–23, but it appears commissioning "plus" was needed. The encounter with Peter tells us a great deal about the repentance and deepening of faith that was needed for him, but perhaps all seven needed this special experience with Jesus to take them over the threshold from confusion and fear to faith.

A Fishy Tale

Jesus got their attention by reenacting a miracle they would remember. Back in the day (Luke 5) Jesus had asked Peter a favor (loan of a boat for preaching purposes), then blessed him with a miracle (huge catch at the wrong time of day), caused him to come face to face with himself (down on his knees) and gave him hope and a future (from now on you will catch men).

Now Peter had gone back to the boat. Did he doubt his usefulness to Jesus? Did he think Jesus had something against him? Did he sense that his denial of Jesus canceled out the commission of Luke 5? Jesus went back to that event to change Peter's mind and heart. This involved pain and vision. It was the pain of his sin that had driven Peter to his knees. It was the vision of Christ that had convinced him to give up his nets.

Pain and Vision

I avoid pain whenever possible—don't we all! But sometimes going back to the place of pain is the only way to make sense of it and move on. There are few more traumatic experiences than being a parent of a child in pain. What makes it worse is standing by helplessly as a doctor treats your child by, necessarily, touching the very spot where the pain exists. When our son was one year old, he fell in the garden and gashed his lip. It was a very bad cut, blood pouring everywhere. We rushed him to the hospital where the wound was sewn up. Can you imagine a hole being sewn up in *your* lip? The poor kid was too young to understand. We had to hold him down by force so the doctor could stick him with the needle repeatedly until the repair was finished. I am not sure if he has forgiven us yet, but it had to be done. The pain of surgery was necessary for the repaired lip to become a reality.

Let me ask the pertinent question, if you don't mind. Is there something you need to revisit? Is Jesus trying to take you somewhere you don't want to go? It is possible to live weeks, months, years, even decades with the nagging knowledge that we need to resolve something with someone or God—and yet not do so. Would Peter have dealt with his issues if left alone? I don't know for sure, but I think he needed Jesus to take the initiative and confront him. Jesus approached Peter so gently. You will notice he did not shout from the shore, "Hi, Pete, it's your old mate Jesus! We need to have a serious talk about the denial thing, especially that final time when you called down curses on yourself and swore you didn't know me!" (Mark 14:71).

No, *first* he helped them out with the big catch, *then* he provided breakfast and *finally* he had the talk with Peter that changed his life. That talk brought both pain and vision. Have you lost God's vision for your life? You can get it back, you can rediscover it, you can rescue it from the attic, dust it off, polish it up—but it is only you that can make the decision to revisit the pain that leads to re-vision.

Peacemaking over Breakfast

If there is something for you to resolve with someone I think it is unlikely God will smack you between the eyes with a wet fish. He is more likely to cook and serve it up to you for breakfast. Perhaps you are thinking, "If God wants me to talk to sister so-and-so, why doesn't he make it obvious?" Or "If my sin *really* needed to be confessed, God would lay such a burden on my heart that I couldn't resist." We are forgetting God wants to *draw* us to him, not beat us about the head! It reminds me of Jeremiah 31:3: "I have loved you with an ever-lasting love; I have drawn you with loving-kindness." What kind of relationship would you rather have with God? It is a *relationship*, after all, and not about *law* or compulsion. No, I reckon God is subtler than we think.

How does this show itself? Here are a few things to ponder: when you pray, are there people you "cannot" pray for? When you are in the fellowship, do you see a brother or sister and have a pang of conscience? When your mobile phone rings and, seeing the caller ID, do you decide not to pick up the call? Now before I send us all on a huge guilt-trip, I should add that there are times to delay diffi-cult conversations. But the key word is *delay*—this is a question of timing, while *avoid* is a question of running away. It must also be acknowledged that despite our best efforts, some people refuse to be reconciled. In this case the lack of reconciliation may still hurt, but the conscience is clear.

To be a disciple of Jesus Christ means to follow and imitate him. He taught peacemaking: "Blessed are the peacemakers, for they will be called sons of God" (Matthew 5:9). He practiced peacemaking among his disciples (Matthew 20:24–28) and between the lost and God (Luke 19:10). He expected his followers to be peacemakers (Matthew 5:23–24). Being a son or daughter of God means, among other things, taking the initiative to reconcile with people we have hurt or have hurt us, helping people reconcile with one another, and helping people be reconciled with God.

The issue is not whether you are the "aggriever" or the "aggrieved," but that you take initiative. This goes to the very heart of the gospel. Jesus came because *he* loved *us*, not because *we* loved *him* (Romans 8:37; Ephesians 5:2; 2 Thessalonians 2:16; 1 John 4:10–11, 19). Our call is to imitate this initiative-taking love. Not an easy teaching, but a counter-cultural, life-changing, world-changing, eternity-destiny-changing teaching. Are you embracing it? Are you praying for the right time, or praying the problem will go away?

Grace and Truth

I have made terrible mistakes as a husband (just ask my wife) and parent (likewise, ask the kids), but this doesn't remove the responsibilities I have to *be* a husband and father. While personal failures dent my confidence, the forgiveness I experience after reconciliation motivates me to try harder to live up to the calling I have received. If I am a better husband and father than I used to be, it is because I am striving to do better, spurred on by the grace granted me. Listen carefully wives, husbands, children, parents, friends, and all who care about people in your lives. I will tell you a secret. If you want people to change, if you want relationships to be transformed bear this in mind:

Grace is more powerful than condemnation.

Don't believe me? Look at how Jesus treated Peter. Pete had been called and commissioned by Christ. He blew it by denial upon denial (18:15–18, 25–27), but this did not change his calling. The message of grace was not fully grasped by Peter, and this obscured the truth about the permanence of his call to be a disciple of Jesus Christ. Peter needed *another* dose of Jesus' grace *and* truth (1:17). Jesus forced Peter to encounter him by taking him back to the time of his calling. Then, once on shore, seated and sated, Jesus proceeded to have the kind of life-changing conversation we all need from time to time. This conversation was hard, even brutal. I don't think Jesus enjoyed it. I am certain Peter didn't. But it was motivated by one thing: the love Jesus had for his friend.

Jesus knew what Peter had done. He knew Peter had grieved over it (Matthew 26:75) and something tells me Peter hadn't quite forgiven himself. I love the touch of detail given us by Mark at the resurrection scene. The angel said to the women,

> "You are looking for Jesus the Nazarene, who was crucified. He has risen! He is not here. See the place where they laid him. But go, tell his disciples *and Peter,* 'He is going ahead of

you into Galilee. There you will see him, just as he told you.'"
(Mark 16:6–7, emphasis mine)

Why this singling out of Peter? I imagine it like this: The women
find the apostles and tell them the first part of the message. Then
there is a pause, the disciples ask, "Is there anything else?"

"Well, there is one other thing," say the women. "He said to tell
the disciples *and Peter*." How does Peter feel when he hears this? The
other apostles and the women turn and look at Pete. There is an
embarrassed silence. People shuffle their feet. Thomas coughs.

"Well, how about that weather?" says Andrew.

Slowly things return to normal. But not for Peter. What do the
angel's cryptic words mean? Is it an olive branch from Jesus? Or is it
a "rub your nose in it" message? Is Jesus saying, "I've still got love in
my heart and hope for your future, Peter. I want to include you and
forgive you"? Or is he saying, "You messed things up Peter, but I
came through. You did your worst but I did my best"? I get the feeling Peter is confused. Sure, he knows Jesus well, but he is also an
emotional and passionate man who cornered the market in the get-
ting-the-wrong-end-of-the-stick game. He is not sure where he
stands with Jesus.

His Lord appearing on the shore excited and worried him. He
was excited about the possibility of full reconciliation. Perhaps
things really could return to the way they were. Could they do a
reenactment of Peter's finest hour (Matthew 16:15–20)? But then he
was also worried this could be another reminder of his guilt. Jesus
gently but firmly led Peter through a process of reminder (that Jesus
had called him, commissioned him and loves him) and then restoration through conversation.

Three times Peter was asked, "Do you love me?" (vv15–17).
Three times Peter said, "Yes." Other than the symbolism of the triple
affirmation of love paralleling the triple denial of friendship
(18:15–18, 25–27), there is a clear call to Peter. What is this call?
The call is to feed the flock. The call is not one of selfishness, self-
focus or self-fulfillment, but one of self-denial and self-sacrifice.

As a friend of mine put it in a thoughtful and challenging book, Jesus is saying, in effect, to Peter,

> "I must be the focus of your attention, not your 'ministry.' Your ministry may—or may not—provide you with fulfillment, but that is not the point. If you focus upon 'being fulfilled,' then you are still preoccupied with yourself. But I have come to call you out of preoccupation with the self. I want you to ground yourself in me, and through that to learn to give yourself away for others."[3]

Frank Gets It Wrong

What a counter-cultural view of religion this is. Not to be in it for what we can get out of it, but to be in it for what we can give others. Now comes the concluding challenge of the whole Gospel of John. Why does the book end on this restoration-confrontation? Why do we have the record of Jesus predicting Peter's death (something that must have happened before John wrote his Gospel and would have been known to his readers)?

As I type this, the music system in the cafe is playing Frank Sinatra's "I Did It My Way" in the background. I heard on a radio program recently that it is the most popular piece of music played at funerals. Is that the best we can say about our lives? That we did it "our way"? Why is that such an honorable thing? If I led my life my way, I know it would be even more of a mess. We can see clearly around us the mess the world is in because humanity lives by this principle.

The end of John's Gospel tells us loudly and clearly that a follower of Jesus, a disciple, a Christian, is called, commissioned and covenanted to follow him. And following means to *be like* the towel-wearing, suffering servant. We are people who do not do life "our way" but "Christ's way," and this way feeds others. It also leads to the cross.

Tertullian, an early church writer, tells us Peter was martyred at Rome, crucified upside down. You and I may never face a physical

---

3. Meic Pearse, *Who's Feeding Whom?* (Paternoster Publishing, Carlisle: Solway, 1996), 17.

wooden cross, but we face spiritual, practical crosses every day (Luke 9:23). John's readership knew Peter's restoration resulted in him living up to his calling. They were being called to the same perseverance, the same faith, the same trust in grace that would result in faithfulness unto death—a faithfulness that would be rewarded with blessings in the next life (Matthew 5:10–12).

Peter was taken to a place of pain so he could live as a man of vision. From this moment forward his life fulfilled the vision Jesus planted within him. He opened the door of the gospel to the Jews (Acts 2), he opened the door of the gospel to the Gentiles (Acts 10 and 11), and he shouted the gospel even more loudly than he had shouted his denials of Christ (Acts 4:8–12, 19–20; 5:29–32, 40–42).

Here is the nearest thing to an altar call you are going to get from me. Please don't let this story, this chapter, this book, this Gospel leave you without you making a decision. Is there a place of pain to revisit? Is there a vision to recapture, or a dream to kindle for the first time? Is there enough in this book for you to take Jesus more seriously than you had before? Is it possible God wanted you to read this book so you could make a decision to become a disciple of Jesus? Just as I haven't written my book aimlessly, neither did John. Perhaps it is good to remind ourselves of his purpose:

> Jesus did many other miraculous signs in the presence of his disciples, which are not recorded in this book. But these are written that you may believe that Jesus is the Christ, the Son of God, and that by believing you may have life in his name. (John 20:30–31)

Have you enjoyed your swim in the elephant's swimming pool? Since you've reached this point in the book, doubtless you have proved Augustine right. You have not drowned! I hope you have learned a few new strokes, improved your stamina for the long-distance swim, or even learned to swim for the first time. Whether you are just getting out of the shallow end or feeling ready to swim the English Channel, I pray this book has pointed you to the swimmer's manual: John's Gospel. Keep swimming, keep learning, keep growing.

Questions for Reflection
1. Do you need to reconcile with someone? What steps can you take to make progress? When will you start?
2. Do you really believe Jesus has totally forgiven you for mistakes you've made in the Christian life? Have you forgiven yourself? Take some time to pray about this.
3. Will you make a promise to Jesus to persevere and feed others? Who can you "feed" today?
4. Is it time to make a decision to get back into the swim or jump in for the first time? Why not make that decision today? Who do you know that can help coach you?

Prayer
Father, thank you for the manna that is your Son. Keep me hungry and thirsty for righteousness and keep me eating and drinking the right food and drink. Give me strength to revisit painful places to find healing for people I love and for myself. Help me to be more interested in feeding others than in being fed. Fill me with faith, the faith I need to follow and keep following. Grant me a life-vision that will transform me into Christ-likeness and that will result in others getting fed with him. I'm grateful you don't count my sins against me. Words are not enough to thank you. I love you. In his name, Amen.

Epilogue

Sink or Swim?

If you have spent any time swimming, you know that thrashing around on the surface gets you nowhere fast. It is exhausting keeping your head out of the water. At some point if you really want to make progress, you have to make a decision to stick your face into the water and get your hair wet. Full immersion is essential to really enjoy the swim. This serves as a metaphor for two purposes.

First, if you are one of those who, having wholeheartedly plunged yourself into the pool of the Christian life, find yourself back splashing around on the surface or, even worse, sitting on the edge of the pool with only your feet dangling in the water, I urge you to get back into the water. I know it might be a shock to the system and that your skin has adjusted to the air temperature and that the water seems awfully cold, but trust me, no, trust God that you'll soon get used to it again and be eternally glad you got back in the swim.

Second, if you have never made the decision to be immersed into Christ (figuratively *and* literally), can I make a suggestion? Trust him, step into the water or just jump right in. You have had a good look at the water, now it is time to get wet! Jesus not only *has* and *is* the water of life; he set us the example by trusting God and being immersed himself (Matthew 3:13–17).

As I write this, it is a week after the twenty-second anniversary of my baptism into Christ. On November 2, 1984, at around 9:30 in the evening I was standing chest-deep in some rather nicely warm water in a baptistery in Bermondsey, South-East London. Next to me stood my friend Chris. Before us were about thirty members of the church. Out of sight but very much present were myriad angels ready to celebrate with joyful songs. Chris asked me some questions; I answered and then descended into the water. I remember looking up and seeing the clear water closing over my head. It seemed as if God's light was shining down on me through the water (I think there was a spotlight in the ceiling directly above the baptistery!).

While under the water I remember thinking, "This is it! This is what my whole life has been leading to and what will make sense of everything between now and when I die. I'm taken from darkness to light, from purposelessness to meaningfulness, from emptiness to fullness. I have found what I'm looking for!" We came up out of the water, the church sang, my heart raced and I resolved to stay in the swim.

These years have seen me sometimes struggling to swim whole-heartedly. At times I have stopped for a while, even spent some time on the edge, but always returned to the water (even if on occasion I have needed a friendly "push" from a friend!). Sometimes I seem to have been swimming against the tide, other times racing along buoyed by a powerful current. In any case, there is no place I would rather be.

The song being sung as I came dripping wet out of the baptistery was "I have decided to follow Jesus, no turning back, no turning back." It is my prayer and determination that I will never turn back.

Do not allow your fear to prevent you from embarking on the most exciting swim imaginable. You see, Jesus is already in the swim, and he is right there ready to help you when you struggle (Matthew 14:25–33).

Come on, get into the water and let's swim together. That elephant needs some company in the deep end.

6